C0-AWH-363

W. H. HUDSON

THE VISION OF EARTH

W. H. HUDSON

W. H. HUDSON

THE VISION OF EARTH

by

ROBERT HAMILTON

KENNIKAT PRESS
Port Washington, N. Y./London

W. H. HUDSON

First published in 1946
Reissued in 1970 by Kennikat Press
Library of Congress Catalog Card No: 76-113336
ISBN 0-8046-1019-3

Manufactured by Taylor Publishing Company Dallas, Texas

He loved birds and green places, and the wind on the heath, and saw the brightness of the skirts of God.

Epitaph on Hudson's grave.

TO MY SONS GERVASE AND ADRIAN

PREFACE

THE study of personality is a task supremely interesting and worth while, above all when it happens to be concerned with genius; for genius is the creator of new ideas and experiences, and the maker of history. But the task is never easy, particularly when the personality is subtle and elusive, as in the case of W. H. Hudson. To have written about him has been a labour of love, a continual enrichment of the writer's mind which it is to be hoped the reader will share; but the wealth and diversity of his outlook, and the discursiveness of his art, have presented many problems. It is impossible to regard him as a naturalist pure and simple, or predominantly as an artist, or even, in the complete sense, a man of letters: he combines within himself elements of all these gifts. Perhaps his own description of himself as a field naturalist 'who takes all life for his field' is the best. Whatever else he may have been, Hudson was a man of profound sensibility. Chalmers Mitchell said that he was 'the most revealing naturalist who has ever lived.' But he was no prophet or proselytizer: the message that emerges from his work is, as one critic put it, 'oblique.' He rarely tells us directly what he believes, hence in order to make his vision clear we must seek to unravel the imperfect concepts through which it is expressed.

I have done what I can to create some sort of order in the pages that follow. First, in The Vision, I have considered the forces, religious, aesthetic, and scientific that influenced Hudson, and their effect upon his attitude to men and birds. I have followed this by a brief sketch of The Man, and of the circumstances that moulded him and gave rise to his vision. Finally, I have dealt with The Work in which the man and his vision were expressed. Hudson's work falls broadly into two sections which I have called Romances and Essays. The Romances comprise a group of novels and short stories, set, for the most part, in South America; and the Essays include travel, nature, and bird books, the majority dealing with English wild life. On the whole, the Romances belong to the earlier period of Hudson's work. The Essays—which are by far the greater part of his output—belong mostly to his middle and later periods. Hence, in taking the Romances first and the Essays afterwards, I have followed a broadly chronological order. The books in each group are treated chronologically, and the chronological order of the whole is preserved in the position of the two books I have selected for separate treatment—the Autobiography, *Far Away and Long Ago*, and *A Hind in Richmond Park*, both of which came at the end of his life, the latter being the last book he ever wrote. Both represent him at the summit of his powers, and in form are somewhat apart from the rest of his work. The Autobiography gives the origins of his vision: the *Hind* is its most complete and explicit expression. The questions raised by the *Hind* bring the book to a conclusion on a return to certain questions which I raised in the first chapter. My aim will have been fulfilled if I have succeeded in revealing something of the nature and value of Hudson's vision, and the quality of his work as a whole.

The status of Hudson's work to-day is assured, and his reputation is high; but he is not a 'popular' author, and it is doubtful if he will ever be very widely read. His most appreciative readers are probably among naturalists and men of letters; and some of the most extravagant praise of his work came from his fellow writers. Perhaps I can express it best by saying that he has a following but not a public. He is not much read abroad, save in the United States and parts of South America, and, in spite of his achievement and the distinction of his personality and style, he cannot be called a universal figure. But it is enough that he was a very great English writer; nor does he lack appreciation in this country. Shortly after his death, the W. H. Hudson Memorial Committee dedicated a noble monument to his memory in the Hyde Park Bird Sanctuary, with its symbolic sculpture of Rima (his best-known creation) by Epstein; and his publishers brought out a more practical monument in the complete edition of his works in twenty-four volumes. 'Few men have left a monument more permanent than Hudson left in his own books,' said Cunninghame Graham. Yet, in spite of his fame, very little has been written about him. The only full-length book is Morley Roberts's *W. H. Hudson: a Portrait*, which is more an intimate memoir than a criticism.

I said, at the outset, that the man of genius is a maker of history; and undoubtedly, within a small field, Hudson changed the world into which he was born. Directly, his effect was not startling; but indirectly, through the spread of his ideals, he is responsible for a great change in the attitude of modern Englishmen. He has made us conscious of nature, and has enriched such consciousness as we already possessed. The remarkable growth of interest in nature books during the last fifty years is largely due to his influence. Yet, though much is read, little is done. The average man reads in order that he may escape for a few hours from the intolerable aridity of industrial life. Nature is, for him, not a wife to be lived with and steadfastly loved, but a mistress, strange, wayward, and beautiful, to be visited from time to time. Always he returns to the partner of his choice—a hard-visaged woman, dirty, drab, and heartless, who grudgingly doles him out pocket-money in return for total servitude and uncreative labour. But it is not only the will that is lacking: another reason—perhaps itself the cause of insufficient will—is the impracticability of settling on the land under modern conditions, in England, at any rate, Hence, what is needed, say the agriculturalists, is a change of social policy. And only where there is a change of heart, say the aesthetics, will a change of policy be possible.

Of those who believed that a change of heart was needed to bring men back to nature, of those who sought to communicate their experience rather than to lay down any practical policy, W. H. Hudson was pre-eminent; and it is through the aesthetic appeal that his effect has been greatest. He did not give us a new religion, or a sociological blue-print. He gave us the vision of earth.

ROBERT HAMILTON.

BEDFORD. 1945.

CONTENTS

THE VISION

No writer possessed a more convinced and deeply held philosophy of life than Hudson, and none ever gave his message so persistently. His conviction that nature is the supreme value, and his message that we must return to nature if life is to be lived integrally and fully, shine from every page he wrote. Yet, paradoxically, he nowhere gives us an explicit statement of what he believes, and never for a moment does he condescend to preach to us. The philosophy and the message are implicit; for he was above all else a man of vision, and his vision was expressed intuitively. My aim in this chapter is, as far as possible, to clarify the meaning of Hudson's vision, and to consider its relation to men and birds, the creatures he loved best. Accordingly the first section of this chapter deals with the psychological origins of his vision, and the religious and aesthetic elements incorporated into it; the second, with the effect of science, and particularly the doctrine of evolution, which played so big a part in his youth; the third, with his relation to man; the fourth, with his relation to birds; and the final section with certain viewpoints that proceeded with cumulative effect from his entire outlook—his realism, faith in life, and so on.

I said that Hudson was, above all, a man of vision. Now vision refers to both the seeing and the thing seen. We often say that a man *has* vision, meaning that he possesses a deeper insight than most people; but we also say that he *sees a vision*, meaning that his insight enables him to behold an aspect of reality that is hidden from others. In this section and the following I shall consider the content of Hudson's seeing, and, in the subsequent sections, its objective aspect.

In all mental vision there is an intensification of consciousness; but the origins of vision are often intuitive and subconscious, and although manifest in and through the imagination, may relate either to sensibility or reason. We hear much of the imaginative sensibility of the artist; but reason can also be imaginative. The artist works up imaginatively his sensuous impressions of sound, colour, shape, and the philosopher works up ideas, and both, through the creative force of what they imagine, leap forward into a higher consciousness; but behind the imagination is the vision—the subconscious intuition of the undiscovered country towards which the imagination moves. I would suggest that the difference between a very clever man and a man of genius is vision, even though the expression of the vision be relatively crude and undeveloped.

The quality of Hudson's vision was primarily aesthetic; but it was balanced by rational and scientific elements. He was saved from the tendency to fanaticism we find in naturists such as Rousseau by his objective attitude. W. P. Witcutt in his book on Jung describes Hudson as primarily an extravert. He was certainly an extravert in the sense that his aim was 'concrete enjoyment,' and his 'morality was similarly orientated.' But his mind was balanced in tension by opposites. Jung himself, while insisting on the importance of types, defines sanity as the development of the potentialities of the whole man. Hudson was very sane. A friend once told him that he was 'too disgustingly sane for anything'; and although, according to Massingham, many people regarded him as an oddity, his apparent oddity proceeded from his sanity which enabled him to be completely himself. He gave full rein to all sides of his nature. His vision derived from a sensitive introspection combined with an extraversion that saved him from ever becoming a 'visionary.'

Like the majority of naturists Hudson was an artist. His sensibility was acute, and he approached nature intuitively and directly rather than rationally and discursively. The naturist is akin to the artist in that both sublimate the brute giveness of materiality: the direct impact of sound, colour, shape, all the multiplicity of the tangible world, is transformed and made significant. It is the scientist who takes the world piecemeal: the naturist receives it whole.

Aesthetic intuition is the mode of Hudson's approach to nature. He does not argue his beliefs with us, for the simple reason that he was not accustomed to argue them with himself; hence the difficulty of defining his intellectual position. I think it was probably akin also to *hylozoism*—the belief that nature, though impersonal, is alive. Hylozoism coloured all the religion of the pagan world, and is implicit in the outlook of primitive societies. It differs from pantheism in deriving from direct, sensuous experience: it is something felt. Pantheism is a philosophy: it postulates as deity everything that exists, including nature as one of the attributes of deity. Again, hylozoism differs not only from philosophic pantheism, but also from scientific materialism; for the materialist regards, not concrete nature, but matter in motion, as the ultimate. A. N. Whitehead distinguishes three great religious concepts: the oriental concept of an impersonal order to which the world conforms (immanence); the Semitic concept of a personal God (transcendence); and the pantheistic concept which regards the ultimate as inclusive of both deity and nature, nature apart from deity being unreal (monism). Hylozoism approaches most closely to immanence, to which is related animism—the personalization of non-human objects. Though Hudson rejected animism with his reason, he felt it deeply in the core of his being, and continually referred to his animistic experiences.

Hudson was one of those instinctive prophets who, without consciously predicting, mirror future tendencies. His vision contained the first intimations of biologism (the modern form of hylozoism). But he also stood for the revolt against mechanist industrialism that developed in the work of the agriculturalists, such as Massingham, Blyton, Henry Warren, and the rest, and assumed such passionate and irrational form in the work of D. H. Lawrence. Naturism can easily lead to the cult of the irrational; but Hudson was far too sane to be lured away by strange experiences. The primitivism and sexual irrationalism of Lawrence and the Nordic cult of blood and soil were alike alien to his spirit. Hudson avoided such excesses. His aesthetic sense took him beyond the sociological agriculturalists, while his scientific temper controlled the excesses of primitivism. In Hudson's vision nature is sublimated in the light of the spiritualized senses. There is no false idealization of nature because nature is seen objectively; nor is there any false materialization of nature because the vision, itself derived from one who is a part of nature, imparts, through him, a transmutation of everything that is seen.

Hudson possessed not only vision, but the gift of expressing it. Vision does not always overflow into utterance or action. Most children have inarticulate vision; and many rare and enlightened minds pass through the world without any wish to express themselves. Others, perhaps the most tragic of all, have a desire for expression incommensurate with their vision. They dream of the great works they might have written, or the great deeds they might have done. We find them in all walks of life—many in asylums, where some strange vision wastes itself in subjective fantasy. The fortunate ones are those in whom greatness of vision is wedded to the full power of expression. When this is the case, whether in the sphere of philosophy, science, literature, or art (or, if the vision relate to action, in the religious or social field), we get true greatness. Now Hudson was articulate in the highest degree. His gift of vision was combined with a creative power which enabled him to communicate the most intimate thoughts and feelings—as in the following passage from *Far Away and Long Ago*, an epitome of his entire outlook and, at the same time, a supreme example of his art. Though written of his childhood in South America, it sums up his whole life.

What, then, did I want?—what did I ask to have? If the question had been put to me then, and if I had been capable of expressing what was in me, I should have replied: I want only to keep what I have; to rise each morning and look out on the sky and the grassy dew-wet earth from day to day, from year to year. To watch each June and July for spring, to feel the same old sweet surprise and delight at the appearance of each familiar flower, every new-born insect, every bird returned once more from the north. To listen in a trance of delight to the wild notes of the golden plover coming once more to the great plain, flying, flying south, flock succeeding flock the whole day long. Oh, those wild beautiful cries of the golden plover! I could exclaim with Hafiz, with but one word changed: 'If after a thousand years that sound should float o'er my tomb, my bones uprising in their gladness would dance in the sepulchre!' To climb trees and put my hand down in the deep hot nest of the Bien-te-veo and feel the hot eggs—the five long-pointed cream-coloured eggs with chocolate spots and splashes at the larger end. To lie on a grassy bank with the blue water between me and beds of tall bulrushes, listening to the mysterious sounds of the wind and of hidden rails and coots and courlans conversing together in strange human-like tones; to let my sight dwell and feast on the *camaloté* flower amid its floating masses of moist vivid green leaves—the large alamanda-like flower of the purest divine yellow that when plucked sheds its lovely petals, to leave you with nothing but a green stem in your hand. To ride at noon on the hottest days, when the whole earth is a-glitter with illusory water, and see the cattle and horses in thousands, covering the plain at their watering-places, to visit some haunt of large birds at that still, hot hour and see storks, ibises, grey herons, egrets of a dazzling whiteness, and rose-coloured spoonbills and flamingoes, standing in the shallow water in which their motionless forms are reflected. To lie on my back on the rust-brown grass in January and gaze up at the wide hot whity-blue sky, peopled with millions and myriads of glistening balls of thistledown, ever, ever floating by; to gaze and gaze until they are to me living things and I, in an ecstacy, am with them, floating in that immense shining void!

In this passage we have the essential Hudson. His sheer objective delight in the visible, tangible world, his vivid sensibility, and the love and acceptance of life, are here perfectly enshrined. When, in his old age, a friend wished him all the New Years he would like to see, he answered: 'That would be a million'; and on another occasion he said that it was natural to cling to life and feel immortal. In these chance remarks we have a revelation of that joy in living, that affirmative note, which imparts so marked a character to all he wrote, and which persisted to the very end. There was no disillusion of old age, only an intensification of experience and an increase of happiness.

Hudson was born into a self-consciously scientific age, and throughout the greater part of his life the scientific climate, operating upon his innate artistic sensibility, helped to shape his beliefs. But although influenced by science, his knowledge was limited, and his natural history not always accurate or up to date. He was, as we have seen, predominantly intuitive and artistic—'author and field naturalist,' to quote the words on his memorial. 'A field naturalist,' he said, 'is an observer of everything he sees.' But his was not primarily the quantitative observation of the scientist: it was far more the qualitative observation of the artist—though perhaps the distinctive thing about him was his synthesis of both quantitative and qualitative, objective and subjective. He saw objectively while at the same time illumining everything he saw in the subjective light of his imagination. His observation combined scientific detachment with intense intuitive perception.

For science, in and for itself, Hudson had little interest. This is not difficult to understand in view of his attitude to nature. Modern science has tended to destroy the living totality of nature. As Whitehead ironically put it, 'nature gets credit which should in truth be reserved for ourselves: the rose for its scent: the nightingale for his song: and the sun for his radiance. The poets are entirely mistaken. They should address their lyrics to themselves, and should turn them into odes of self-congratulation on the excellency of the human mind. Nature is a dull affair, soundless, scentless, colourless; merely the hurrying of material, endlessly, meaninglessly.' And in view of the fact that many scientists believe that the mind itself is material, it is but a short step to the abolition of man as well as nature.

This scientific emasculation of nature and man was utterly alien to Hudson's outlook. For him, scientific knowledge was subordinate to the concrete experience of nature, and its purpose was mainly the clarification of the understanding in order that a greater and profounder experience might be enjoyed. Science, like magic to which it is related, seeks to subdue nature to man. In the words of C. S. Lewis: 'For the wise men of old the cardinal problem had been how to conform the soul to reality, and the solution had been knowledge, self-discipline, and virtue. For magic and applied science alike the problem is how to subdue reality to the wishes of men . . .' Thus Hudson's attitude to nature was much more akin to religion than to science.

Lewis emphasizes applied science; but it is mainly in analysis that science has carried the destructive process farthest. The analytical branches of science, astronomy, chemistry, and physics (those mainly of which Whitehead is thinking), have progressed out of all proportion to the synthetical branches, biology and psychology; but they follow a dwindling path. Astronomy reduces vast, complex areas of matter to their simplest constituents: chemistry analyses these constituents into simpler elements; and physics analyses these elements into their ultimate properties. Conversely, biology and psychology tend to interpret life increasingly as a synthesis of parts in a greater whole. Both branches, analytical and synthetical, in their ultimate aspect approach the domain of metaphysics. At one end physics analyses matter into the ontological realm: at the other end psychology, in its attempt to create a synthesis, passes over into a form of epistemological speculation. The analytical sciences do not give us any information about nature in Hudson's sense of the word. Information as to the distance and size of stars, the composition of metals, and the structure of atoms tells us nothing about nature as Hudson *experienced* it; but (leaving aside psychology which can never be a science at all in the strict sense, since the human mind must always elude rigid demonstration) we shall find that, of the synthetic sciences, biology alone approaches to a description of nature as given in experience.

Biology, which means the science of life, does lead—within the limits of scientific method—towards a genuine view of nature as a whole; but it also tends towards the conception of a self-sufficient universe, and its influence upon the age in which Hudson grew up partly explains his attitude to religion. The editor of a famous periodical once remarked that biology seems more productive of religious unbelief than the analytical and relatively mechanized branches of science. But I suggest that this is what we should expect. The mechanical activity revealed by physics, astronomy, and chemistry, is so inadequate to explain our concrete experience of the richness and multiplicity of life that we tend to postulate a creative mind to account for it. As Professor Arthur Thomson pointed out, the whole point about a machine is that it is something *made*. In astronomy there is also the emotion of awe. We are more likely to find God at the end of a telescope than at the end of a microscope. But for the biologist, dealing with living things, nature seems itself to be its own sufficient explanation. As he proceeds downwards, even the most primitive forms reveal some life; 'therefore,' he concludes, 'if I could discover the conditions, all matter would be, in a sense, living.' And, as he proceeds upwards, he beholds an increasing synthesis of the parts of living matter resulting in a continual growth towards higher forms; hence he tends to conclude that the universe is self-sufficient.

It is easy to see the relation of biologism to hylozoism. Of all departments of science, biology is most in harmony with intuitive naturism, and, as such, exercised considerable influence upon Hudson. The great scientific revolution of his youth was in biology, and its driving force was the theory of evolution which, viewing life as a self-unfolding unity, seemed to give objective support to his own instinctive hylozoism.

To-day, when 'the noise of the battle of evolution' has died down, and only a distant rumble of controversy reaches us from afar, it is difficult to enter into the partisan feelings aroused in Hudson's youth. It was not so much the fact of evolution itself that aroused such bitter feelings: evolution had been in the air for generations, and had been foreshadowed by many of the Fathers of the Church: it was the doctrine of natural selection that gave offence, and there were many who, like Hudson, regarded it as incompatible with religious belief, mainly on three grounds. Natural selection seemed to make the universe the result of chance, to reduce life to a mechanism, and involve endless time and wastage, spatial insignificance, and pain. Hudson, while never fully accepting natural selection as the only and final mode of evolution, found it destructive of revealed religion on these grounds. Much as I respect his judgment, it seems to me that he could never have fully thought out the meaning and implications of the argument.

Chance is commonly conceived as an entirely unrelated series of happenings. But, in fact, what we usually call 'chance' is really the result of rigid law. When we look at an event atheistically we call it 'chance,' and when we look at it theistically we say it is willed, entirely overlooking the fact that in either case it is *determined*—either intrinsically, or by God. Although modern physics seems to have opened the way for genuine chance, science as a whole reveals universal law; and even if we say that electronic events are fortuitous, the atomic wholes in which they combine give us concrete unities subject to ascertainable law; and furthermore, we have reason to believe that even the so-called indeterminacy of electronic events may be due less to the events observed than to our own inadequacy in observing them. The universe as we experience it is clearly determined by law, and our conception of chance is really a misconception. Yet even on grounds of chance, it has always seemed to me strange that those who criticize natural selection for getting rid of God, should willingly accept the paradox of fortuitous and divine creation in individual birth. Thus a man and a woman meet, as so often happens, quite by chance: they fall in love and get married, and nobody will deny that their child is the result of this chance meeting; but the believer will say that the soul of the child is the direct creation of God, thus accepting both chance and creation. Where, then, is the difficulty of believing that the universe has unrolled from a cloud of gas by chance, and that the soul of Adam was directly created by God?

The mechanical process of natural selection stood greatly in the way of religious belief in Hudson's youth; yet mechanism is, if anything, more favourable to a theistic explanation of the universe than vitalism, since the former demands a maker while vitalism tends to make the universe self-sufficient.

Hudson was inclined to be sceptical of the part played by chance and mechanism in evolution: what chiefly impressed him was the length of time and wastage, the spatial insignificance, and the pain. The problem of time in evolution is really a pseudo-problem; for time is extrinsic to the infinite-eternal God, and no criterion based upon either brevity or length can be used in criticism of the theocentric position. From a human standpoint it may seem difficult to believe that the Creator should have brought into being a vast cosmic process of unthinkable length in order to produce one species on a relatively minute globe; but once we realize that time is extrinsic to God it becomes irrelevant whether man was formed from 'the slime of the earth' in a single moment or from a cloud of gas in millions of years. The incongruity is in us, and cannot be applied to a timeless being. So also with our spatial insignificance, which we contrast, in imagination, with the vast, overwhelming cosmos. Imagination revolts at the picture; but reason comes to our aid with the thought that since it is in the *mind* of this physically insignificant creature that the contrast exists, the very notion of his insignificance in space and time witnesses to his significance in reality.

Concerning the problem of pain we are on more difficult ground. Hudson, watching the ichneumon flies who paralyse the bodies of their victims so that their grubs may be able to feed on live flesh, asks: 'How reconcile these facts with a beneficent Creator who designed it all?' And he goes on to attempt to answer his own question:

> It is curious to see now that Darwin himself gave the first comfort to those who, convinced against their will, were anxious to discover some way of escape which would not involve the total abandonment of their cherished beliefs. At all events, he suggested the idea, which religious minds were quick to seize upon, that the new explanation of the origin of the innumerable forms of life which people the earth from one or a few primordial organisms afforded us a nobler conception of the creative mind than the traditional one. It does not bear examination, probably it originated in the author's kindly and compassionate feelings rather than in his reasoning faculties; but it gave temporary relief and served its purpose. Indeed, to some, to very many perhaps, it still serves as a refuge—this poor, hastily made straw shelter, which lets in the rain and wind, but seems better to them than no shelter at all.

But of the intentionally consoling passages in the book, the most impressive to me was that in which he refers to instincts and adaptations such as those of the wasp, which writers on natural history subjects are accustomed to describe, in a way that seems quite just and natural, as *diabolical.* That, for example, of the young cuckoo ejecting its foster-brothers from the nest; of slave-ants, and of the larvae of the Ichneumonidae feeding on the live tissues of the caterpillars in whose bodies they have been hatched. He said that it was not perhaps a logical conclusion, but it seemed to him more satisfactory to regard such things 'not as specially endowed or created instincts, but as small consequences of one general law'—the law of variation and the survival of the fittest.

This passage throws a good deal of light on Hudson's attitude. Although for years he had clung to the vague form of Christianity he had learned, very inadequately, in his childhood, he gradually abandoned it; and when, towards the end of his life, he wrote *The Book of a Naturalist* from which the passage is taken, all orthodox belief had gone. But there was no arrogant disbelief; only regret for a position he could no longer hold. We see, however, that it was not so much the comfort given by Darwin that was illogical as Hudson's reaction to it. If he had been more of a philosopher he would have seen the defect both in Darwin's attempt at comfort (which seems to have been genuine enough since, judging by Darwin's life and correspondence, he seems never to have given up the theistic position) and his own reaction. Neither a 'beneficent Creator,' nor blind mechanism will solve the problem of pain; but pain is at least explained by the first, whereas the second leaves it naked in all its irrational horror. The theistic solution can be expressed by saying that every living being from amoeba to man, from man to archangel, must, as less than God, suffer from the limitations of its nature, from which it can only be released by a striving which itself involves suffering; but Hudson's intuitive naturism, his unphilosophical mind, and the kind of Christianity in which he was reared, prevented him from ever coping with the problem from this angle.

The chief argument against materialistic evolution is the impossibility of an evolving reason—an argument invariably shirked by materialists. Chesterton argued that we can demonstrate man's spiritual distinction from the animals from the evidence of the primitive cave drawings, since no animal has ever attempted to express itself in art. But it is just possible for art gradually to have evolved out of an intensified and brightened sense life; and many of the higher animals have a rudimentary sense of beauty. What, I submit, is impossible is the evolution of the power to think 'Things that are equal to the same thing are equal to one another,' or 'I think, therefore I am.' Such ideas are *sui generis*, and have no origin in any lower mental state. It would be painful to watch the mental gymnastics of any one who attempted to show how the power to think such ideas could have evolved materially. Conceptual thought, not the sense of beauty, is the proof of man's uniqueness in the evolutionary scheme: the missing link is mental, not physical. This kind of argument, however, would have made little appeal to Hudson, who temperamentally underrated the place of reason, and had no aptitude for metaphysical thought.

I have gone into the problems of evolution at some length because of their effect upon Hudson's vision and their incorporation into his work. To-day these problems are in the melting-pot, and no man can tell what will emerge; but the present relation between religion and science (as we see from the remarkable syntheses of orthodox Christianity and evolution by Dr. Messenger and Canon de Dorlodot) is a portent. Unfortunately the Christianity in which Hudson was reared did not equip him to stand up to the challenge of evolution: the purely negative questions, such as time, wastage, and pain, left him bewildered. On the positive side we may say that his mind instinctively tended towards the acceptance of complete evolutionism, i.e. the doctrine of the growth of the human mind from lowlier forms without any supernatural intervention; and when, after many years, he came to hold that doctrine fully, he embraced something which was the scientific complement of what he had always instinctively believed.

Hudson's acceptance of evolution was more felt than reasoned. He was neither irrational nor an 'irrationalist'; but emotion and imaginative sensibility held primacy for him. He saw the life of nature intensifying in the evolving sensibility of animal life, and culminating in the emotional and imaginative powers of man. The doctrine of evolution confirmed his conviction of the need for an earth-life sublimated and purified in the crucible of the human mind.

For Hudson, evolution revealed the unity of nature and the place of man as part of nature. But man, though one in kind with the earth that had begotten him, was set a little apart by the quality of his mind: he was the mirror in which nature attained self-consciousness. As the saint loves man in God, so Hudson loved man in nature; and though his affection was tempered by detachment and often hidden under reserve, he inspired a genuine affection in others. It was, I think, Morley Roberts who suggested that his epitaph, 'He loved birds and green places,' should be changed to 'He loved birds and *man*.' His books are, it is true, centred in nature; but for him, nature included human nature in all its fullness and richness. 'My credentials,' he writes in his last book, *A Hind in Richmond Park*, 'are those of a field naturalist who has observed men: all their actions and their mentality'; and it was the detachment of the observing field naturalist allied to a genuine sympathy that gave him so clear and realistic a view of man.

In *Man and Literature* Norman Nicholson considers three contemporary views of man: Liberal Man, Natural Man, and Imperfect Man. The first is the view of the humanitarian progressive; the second, of the primitive; the third, of the Christian who sees man as a fallen being in need of redemption. But it does not follow that the redemptive view must necessarily be Christian. Hudson saw man as fallen and in need of redemption; but it was from nature that he had fallen, and it was through nature that he was to be redeemed. This redemption did not mean a return to the jungle but to nature enriched by the creative imagination. For not only is human life enriched by contact with nature: nature is enriched by the impact of man's creativity. Jane and Maxwell Fry have pointed out that 'There are few countries in the world that man has not in some way altered, and the English countryside is of all countries the most man-made'; and it was the English countryside that Hudson loved best of all. No one has ever captured its quality more perfectly, or gathered into one focus more effectively its intimate relation of man and landscape. Nature is not complete, and therefore not nature at all but a mere abstraction, without man; nor is it given to any man, even the most ardent lover of primitive wildness, to separate nature from himself. Hudson did not ask us to renounce our humanity and return to the empty desert waste and the dark primeval forest. He sang, rather, of earth beautified in the light of a human sensibility which itself derives from earth and enriches it a thousandfold.

Hudson had no facile blue-print for a perfect world. He sketched the lines on which man might achieve integration in nature, and left it at that. It has been suggested that *A Crystal Age* is his Utopia, and it is true that, in spite of elements of exaggeration and fantasy, this strange, imperfect book does embody many of Hudson's hopes for a better world; but we must take it with many reservations. Thus he writes of a time when

most of the things most valued have been consumed to ashes—politics, religion, systems of philosophy, isms and ologies of all descriptions; schools, churches, prisons, poorhouses; stimulants and tobacco; kings and parliaments; cannon with its hostile roar, and pianos that thundered peacefully; history, the Press, vice, political economy, money, and a million things more.

Hudson is exaggerating; yet it may plausibly be maintained that many of the things listed could disappear from the world, leaving us none the worse and in many ways much better. A devastating series of wars on the scale of the last two might easily destroy civilization completely, forcing men back to a medieval condition in which the worship of God and the cultivation of the earth became the supreme ends of life. Such a world might be an improvement on our own, not in terms of material comfort, but of integration.

A Crystal Age contains certain passages that suggest some curious speculations on the place of sexuality in human life; but here again we must not regard Hudson's fantasy as an explicit statement of his beliefs. His Utopians are divided up into small communities, each community replenished by a single person, the Mother, as in the bee-hive. But the members of the community are not at all like bees. They are individual personalities with great powers of imagination, and with deep affections which bind them together freely on the family pattern. The range and satisfaction of their lives transcend the sexual instinct, in its grosser aspect at all events, and leave them free to develop all sides of their nature. Hudson seems to imply that a full life in which all the senses are lifted to a higher plane, an aesthetic life in harmony with nature, would considerably reduce the force of the sexual instinct. Whether this is true or not, it is certain that the sheer uncreativeness and frustration of industrial life increases the sexual urge. The threat to the ego caused by the insecurity of industrial life is compensated by an increase of sexuality—for there is reason to believe, on Adlerian grounds, that excessive sexuality is the masquerade of a hidden and frustrated will to power. At the same time, the mechanical character of industrialism directly fosters the artificiality which is a breeding-ground of sexual neurosis. Normal sexuality is creative, and centred in the family; but, as a psychologist put it, anomalous sexuality tends to be *mechanical* in content. Again, the fact that the modern industrial worker is propertyless undermines personal responsibility and disintegrates the family; and with the break-up of family life the natural checks on the sexual instinct are removed. Karl Otten has pointed out that wherever totalitarianism is powerful, increased sexual licence is substituted for decreased political responsibility. The totalitarian ideal of 'the greatest freedom in the sexual sphere and none at all in the political,' is implicit in every industrial society, whether totalitarian or otherwise. Finally, the frustration of artistic expression in industrial society leads to a starvation of the senses and to a corresponding increase of sexuality. It may be that Hudson overrated the force of the sexual instinct, and this probably led him to exaggerate the necessity for its transcendence—as when he wrote: 'there is no millennium, no rest, no perpetual peace till that fury has burnt itself out.' The modern tendency to give too much importance to the sexual instinct—a tendency which, in itself, increases it—has been fostered, not only by our artificial industrial environment, but by psychoanalysis, and by the modern novel as typified in the work of Lawrence.

We may agree with Hudson that the fuller cultivation of the other senses and instincts would lessen the force of sexuality. But our knowledge of the other instincts is very limited, and we tend to reduce them to two or three only. C. A. Claremont has argued, in *The Innumerable Instincts of Man*, that we possess a great number of instincts, each directed to a different end. It is impossible to go into his argument here, but his book should be read by any one interested in Hudson—a man who refused to be bound by any arbitrary science of the mind or of nature, and who saw life as an immense and complex overflow of creativity.

The most tragic thing about modern industrial society is its frustration. Some have rebelled, and sought violently to overthrow it: others, like Hudson, have turned their backs upon it altogether, seeking their own free life. But non-co-operation tends to play into the hands of the totalitarian forces and allows them to increase; and unless we discover some large-scale organization to counteract industrial totalitarianism there can be little hope of improvement. It is here that the more political-minded agriculturalists can help us, and it is to them that we must look for a practical lead.

There are, however, some individuals who, by their calling and mission, are best divorced from political life; and of such was Hudson. His vision was beyond politics: it related more to the realm of art and mysticism—and this, I think, accounts for his lack of interest in the practical side of naturism for which Massingham, Blyton, Henry Warren, and others are so enthusiastic. The means interested him less than the end. He beheld a vision of man united with the living earth of which he was the highest part; but how that unity was to be achieved in an industrial and increasingly totalitarian world he did not ask. Yet without the right means there can be no satisfactory end. As Middleton Murry has observed, 'if beauty is ever to be restored to the national life it can only be by restoring the reverence for the earth.' But 'a vital distinction has to be made: between a contemplative and an active reverence. There is plenty of contemplative reverence for the Earth': 'the reverence for the Earth we need . . . is the active reverence that is expressed in cultivating it with an instinctive regard for its own sovereign and independent life . . .'

Hudson's 'contemplative reverence for the Earth' (the necessary inspiration to the men of action who came after him) explains his conservatism. 'So far as Hudson was anything in politics he was Conservative,' said Morley Roberts. Now conservatism is, as Disraeli showed, based upon reverence for the soil; and it is a noteworthy fact that totalitarian movements arise wherever there is a tendency to sweep away the traditions of the past, and to concentrate on an increased urbanization. Hudson was conservative: he was not *a* Conservative in the sense of being a party man. 'I don't understand politics,' he confessed to Roberts. 'And, therefore,' Roberts answered, 'are a rabid Conservative'—a remark that reveals the truth that Conservatism is more a traditional way of life than a political system. Another reason for Hudson's conservatism was his individualism. The individual, the family, and the small community are the safeguards of tradition and, as such, the preservers of liberty which proceeds from tradition; but they are stifled in an industrial society which necessarily leads to mass action and regimentation, and to the abstract idea of man with which socialism is impregnated. In the chapter on sheep in *The Book of a Naturalist* Hudson satirizes the socialist Utopia:

> A sheep cannot 'follow his own genius,' so to speak, without infringing the laws we have made for his kind. His condition in this respect is similar to that of human beings under a purely socialistic form of government: for example, like that of the ancient civilized Peruvians. In that state every man did as he was told: worked and rested, got up and sat down, ate, drank, and slept, married, grew old and died in the precise way prescribed. And I daresay if he tried to be original or to do something out of the common he was knocked on the head.

All forms of regimentation were abhorrent to Hudson. An original in himself, he was attracted by originality in others—the quality of strangeness that is becoming increasingly rare in the modern world. There is a wide distinction between the words strangeness and eccentricity. The former relates to normal individuality: the latter to abnormal. Both words are, to some extent onomatopoeic. Strangeness has the musical sound associated with the mystery of personality: eccentricity, the angular sound of distortion and comic egoism. Hudson himself was a strange being. Pre-eminently sane, he yet stood apart from his fellows in some indefinable way. To be fully and integrally oneself is never easy, for the experience of individuality which we all possess is inevitably accompanied by a sense of isolation from the vast, overshadowing power of the not-self, and gives rise to the desire to lose the self in a crowd. Hence, the natural individuality we bring into the world is lost through fear, and the standardized man, pathetically ignorant of the fact that the crowd with which he shouts is composed of individuals just as lonely and just as eager to shout with the crowd as himself, is the result. The exponents of the idea of mass-humanity tend to confuse individuality with egoism. But egoism is the worship, the 'making absolute' (in Allers's words) of one's individuality. Genuine individuality derives from the integration of the ego in the service of an ultimate value conceived of as greater than the ego. For Hudson, this ultimate value was nature, in which his individuality was reflected and integrated. His love of the original extended to the whole organic world. The strange, elusive serpent fascinated him, and references to serpents recur continually throughout his work. But it was the original in human life that attracted him most; and the odd and incongruous gave him an outlet for his quiet, but wholly effective and satisfying humour.

Although he had so genuine an affection for his fellow men, Hudson seems to have lacked the capacity for great love or profound psychological understanding. His concrete, vivid, extraverted acceptance of nature as a whole, made his approach to the complexities of human nature somewhat limited. Such sympathy and understanding as he possessed seem to have originated from neither purely spiritual nor purely psychological sources, but from a simple and direct intuition. There are three kinds of men who get on with their fellows: those who love them out of spiritual charity; those who possess a wide psychological knowledge of human nature in all its fullness; and those who, like Hudson, without great spiritual understanding or psychological knowledge, are direct and uninhibited in their approach. Man plays a predominant part in Hudson's work, and no understanding of his vision is possible apart from man in whom it attains completeness. His approach to human nature contains elements of great value for our mechanical age; and if more of us could see our fellow man simply and directly as Hudson saw him, there might be a greater hope for the future.

After man, the creatures who live most vividly in Hudson's work are birds. Many have had a greater love and a profounder understanding of man; but none have so loved and understood birds. This understanding—a unique gift that set him apart from all his contemporaries—did not conflict with, but enriched his human contacts. *Birds and Man*, the title of one of his books, might well be the title of them all; for in everything he wrote, in whatever sphere, birds and man are never far away. There is, indeed, as Charles Morgan has pointed out, an intimate relation between them. 'It is not,' he writes, 'an emotional exaggeration, but simply true, to say that birds have upon man an influence of purification and redemption. In his darkest hour, when it seems to him that his own kind has spread a blight over the whole world, they are for him a visible reassurance to the contrary.' It may be that this intimate relation partly derives from resemblance: from the fact that, like men, birds stand upright on their two legs, and are artists of a sort—builders and musicians. As Hudson puts it in *Adventures among Birds*:

they are vertebrates and relations, with knowing, emotional, thinking brains like ours in their heads, and with senses like ours, only brighter. Their beauty and grace, so much beyond ours, and their faculty of flight which enables them to return to us each year from such remote outlandish places, their winged swift souls in winged bodies, do not make them uncanny but only fairy-like. Thus we love and know them, and our more highly developed minds are capable of bridging the gulf which divides us from them, and divides bird from mammal.

Their nearness to man, coupled with the remote 'fairy-like' quality of which Hudson speaks, gives them their unique charm. To my mind, this quality of nearness-remoteness is the secret of all charm; of the charm that, far beyond any biological attraction, men find in women and women in men, and the charm of children. Hudson, as we have seen, was very susceptible to the quality of strangeness which itself proceeds from the quality of nearness-remoteness. In his many portraits of women and children he captures this quality; but it is in writing of birds that he captures it most successfully. The predatory hawk, the impudent jackdaw, the gentle willow wren—all were touched with a magic that brought out to the full their strangeness and charm.

When Hudson first began to write, towards the end of the last century, there was little interest in birds for their own sake: the people most interested were scientists, sportsmen, and collectors. Hudson's advocacy for the protection of birds, and the aesthetic effect of his books, did much to make us conscious of their charm; and the enormous growth of interest, as revealed by bird-watching clubs, books, articles, and wireless talks, is largely due to his influence. Although a rather unpractical man in every-day life, he was practical in his championship of birds. His work for the Society for the Protection of Birds was unremitting, and he gave generously out of his small earnings.

Birds were symbolic of all that was brightest in Hudson's vision—symbolic in their beauty, freedom, and vividness of sensation, and, above all, their intense activity and abundant life. He wanted men to learn from the birds; to bring the superior intellectual and spiritual gifts of the human mind more close to the avian. He himself possessed a unique power of entering into the bird-mind. Birds alone among non-human creatures possess the power of utterance to any advanced degree; and song is the key to the minds, not only of the song-birds, but to the bird-mind as a whole. Hudson realized how intimately song expresses the bird-mind, and his books are full of sensitive interpretations of this elusive music. One of the finest examples is his chapter on the blackbird in *Adventures among Birds*. It is not surprising that, like so many other lovers of birds, he was peculiarly attracted to the blackbird's song, a song unique in quality and character. The quality is exceptionally pure and clear, with a strange, tremulous sound at times, while in character the song differs from that of all other birds in the freedom and range of its extemporizations and in its phrases of a recognizable musical pattern. But, according to Hudson, 'this character of the blackbird's music—its resemblance to human-made music—is not the whole nor the principal cause of its charm.'

The charm is chiefly due to the intrinsic beauty of the sound; it is a fluty sound and has that quality of the flute suggestive of the human voice, the voice in the case of the blackbird of an exquisitely pure and beautiful contralto. The effect is greatly increased by the manner in which the notes are emitted—trolled out leisurely, as if by a being at peace and supremely happy, and able to give the feeling its most perfect expression.

The peaceful and supremely happy quality of which Hudson speaks is found in no other British bird, and to capture it at its best one should listen late in the evening, when other birds are silent. Heard at the close of a long June day, the blackbird seems to sum up all the splendour and serenity of summer in a voice. His cousin, the ring-ouzel, closely resembles him; but the environment of the two birds is very different, and the songs vary accordingly. Hudson observes of the ring-ouzel's song that 'its charm is mainly due to the place you hear it in, the wildness and solitude of the rocky glens or the mountain's side.' In other words, it expresses the character of its environment.

I first drew attention to this question of environment and song some years ago, under a pseudonym, in a now defunct nature journal. Environmental relationship cuts across family relationship, and we often find closely related birds, such as the blackbird and ring-ouzel, whose songs have a distinct family relationship, differing chiefly in the expression of their environment: the one serene and full, reflecting his sylvan background, the other wild and free, in keeping with his moors and hills. That family relationship in song exists is undeniable: thus the thrushes and heir relatives are distinguished by purity of quality, and a declamatory character—a series of short, recitative-like passages with a pause between each, ranging from the variability of the blackbird, through the stereotyped repetitions of the song thrush, to the desultory soliloquy of the robin; the warblers by brightness of quality, and flowing conversational character, like a rapidly spoken sentence, beginning with a preposition and ending with a conjunction; the titmice by thin, metallic notes, and short, metrical phrases; larks and pipits by rapid, continuous music; and so on. (There are, of course, many exceptions, notably among the large and widespread finch family.) Now it is by no means improbable that the variations of song within each family, and to a lesser extent between one family and another, are caused by environment. If we divide environment broadly into woodlands, marshes, heaths, moorlands, and the sea, we shall notice that the richness and clarity of the songs of woodland birds is the perfect expression of their sylvan environment, while birds of the marshland and places where water and reeds abound express the character of their surroundings in a rapid, liquid, reedy chatter: heath birds usually have harsh, brief songs (or, more often, sub-songs) that are peculiarly in harmony with the character of sand, stone, heath, and furze; and the lonely piping of moorland birds, and the wild screams of sea birds, have an uncanny fitness to their surroundings. And if it be asked how all this has come about, I would suggest that the songs of woodland birds have developed their serenity and technical elaboration largely on account of the protection afforded by their environment; and I think that exposure to varying degrees of hardship, and the power of mimicry, go far towards explaining the environmental character of the other groups. Birds are notoriously good mimics, and the chatter of marsh birds might easily be explained by the sound of running water and the movement of reeds and sedges, the brief chirps and twitterings of heath birds by the spasmodic noises of the heath, such as the chirping of crickets and the crackling of furze, the piping of moorland birds by the song of the wind in long grass, and the screams of sea birds by the everlasting dialogue of wind and wave. There are exceptions, such as the skylark and the curlew, both occupying a very exposed environment and, at the same time, having elaborate and highly developed songs; but their great power on the wing gives them an advantage over their enemies, and puts them into the category of 'protected' species on a par with the woodland birds. (Flight and song together is usually inhibited by the fact that most great songsters are woodland species, and their capacity for flight during the song season is limited to short, vertical flights within the territory). The many problems arising out of family and environmental relationship are of great importance, and their solution may well be the key to understanding the evolution of song. I would suggest that we do actually see, or hear, the evolution of song at work on these lines in the genus *sylvia*. All the songs of this genus reveal the family character and rhythm: the distinctions derive from environment. The Dartford warbler, dwelling on heaths and commons, sings the primitive, basic song of the genus—a mere speeding up of the harsh call-note, a throaty chatter—which, in the more protected greater whitethroat, is improved and polished, and in the woodland-dwelling garden warbler and blackcap, finally perfected.

I have touched on this question of family relationship and environment, not only because of its intimate bearing upon Hudson's sensitive recordings of song, but in order that the reader may grasp the background to the subject and deepen his appreciation of Hudson. In song he found the key to the understanding of birds. No one has so perfectly captured this enchanting music, and it is to be hoped that someone will make a 'Hudson Bird-Song Anthology,' bringing together all his marvellous writings on the subject.

Hudson's approach to song was primarily aesthetic and intuitive; and the same may be said of his attitude to bird life as a whole. His purely scientific knowledge of ornithology was not great; yet he succeeded in telling us more about birds than the most learned experts. He was able to enter into the bird mind because he *loved* birds, and possessed avian qualities in his own mind and character: even his appearance—tall, gaunt, bearded, with small, bright, observant eyes—had in it something bird-like. He looked at times, said one of his friends, 'like a huge raptorial.' The identification of his own mind with the birds' is brought out in a wonderful passage from *Adventures among Birds*, describing a newly-arrived migrant redwing on the seashore; and it is song that opens the well-springs of his imagination:

> Now as I rested there against the pile of brushwood on which he sat so near me he continued to emit these soft low chirping notes or little drops of musical sound; and it seemed in part a questioning note, as if he was asking me what I was? Why I regarded him so attentively? What were my intentions towards him? And in part it was a soliloquy, and this was how I interpreted what he appeared to be saying: 'What has come to me—what ails me that I cannot continue my journey? The sun is now as high as it will be: the green country is so near—a few minutes' flight would carry me across this flat sea-marsh to the

woods and thickets where there are safety and the moist green fields to feed in. Yet I dare not venture. Hark! that is the hooded crow; he is everywhere roaming about over the marshland in quest of small crabs and carrion left by the tide in the creeks. He would detect this weakness I find in me which would cause me to travel near the surface with a languid flight; and if he saw and gave chase, knowing me to be a sick straggler, my heart would fail and there would be no escape. Day and night I have flown southward from that distant place where my home and nest was in the birches, where with my mate and young and all my neighbours we lived happily together, and finally set out together on this journey. Yesterday when it grew dark we were over the sea, flying very high; there was little wind, and it was against us, and even at a great height the air seemed heavy. And it grew black with clouds that were above us, and we were wetted with heavy rain; it ceased and the blackness went by, and we found that we had dropped far, far down and were near the sea. It was a quiet sea, and the sky had grown very clear, sprinkled with brilliant stars as on a night of frost, and the stars were reflected below us so that we seemed to be flying between two starry skies, one above and one beneath. I was frightened at that moving, black, gleaming sky beneath me, and felt now that I was tired, and when the flock rose higher and still higher I laboured to rise with it. At intervals those who were leading uttered cries to prevent the others from straggling, and from far and near there were responsive cries; but from the time that the dark, wetting cloud had come over us I uttered no sound. Sometimes I opened my beak and tried to cry, but no cry came; and sometimes as we flew my eyes closed, then my wings, and for a moment all sensation was lost, and I would wake to find myself dropping, and would flutter and struggle to rise and overtake the others. At last a change came, a sudden warmth and sense of land, a solid blackness instead of the moving, gleaming sea beneath us, and immediately we dropped earthwards like falling stones, down into the long grass by the shore. Oh, the relief it was to fold my wings at last, to feel the ground under me, the close, sheltering stems around and over me, to shut my tired eyes and feel no more!

'When morning came, the cries of my fellows woke me: they were calling us up and going away over the marshes to the green country; but I could not follow nor make any response to their calls. I closed my eyes again, and knew no more until the sun was high above the horizon. All were gone then—even my own mate had left me; nor did they know that I was hidden here in the grass seeing that I had not answered to the call.'

We may feel that this is a piece of artistic self-projection; yet it seems to ring true. The intense, patient observation with which Hudson watches the tired and lonely bird, and the profound sympathy with which he interprets its anxious, questioning notes, overreaches the barrier between the human and the bird mind, and we seem to feel with the redwing something of the fear, the exhaustion, the mystery and ecstasy of that long migration. Hudson's language is human enough, and he probably polished it in the writing; but the emotion it captures and expresses is, we instinctively feel, genuine. Those 'soft, low, chirping notes' when they fell upon Hudson's ear in that lonely place, struck upon the door of his imagination, and awakened in him a sympathy which was long afterwards recaptured and set down in this great and moving passage.

Hudson thought of bird-life as the ideal to which man, with his superior faculties, should approximate; and, indeed, if nature is accepted as the ultimate value, it follows that an intense and spiritualized life of the senses is the highest to which man can attain. But such a view, with all its beauty and appeal to the heart, suffers from very grave limitations. At best it is incomplete: at worst, deficient. The vision of earth needs to be completed in the vision of the living God—and it was here that Hudson failed. Such beliefs as he retained were, as we have seen, conventional: for him nature was the ultimate reality. Yet at its brightest, his vision transcends its limitations and enters into the realm of the eternal. In spite of his excessive love of the tangible, living world, the naturist does, at rare moments, make contact with the infinite and eternal; and it was in such moments that Hudson saw God.

This illumination—plus his native sanity—saved him from the pessimism that would otherwise have proceeded from the limitations of his outlook; for the extent of our hope depends on the breadth of our vision. It is obvious that one who lives for himself alone cannot be other than discouraged, absorbed as he is in the limitation and insignificance of his ego; but he who lives for his property, or family, or country, or art, is not much better off. The humanitarian whose vision extends to the whole race of men has a wider ground for hope; and the naturist, whose vision includes man and all the values subsumed under man as part of nature, approaches still more nearly to the absolute hope which alone derives from God. But any ultimate value less than God contains, *as* less than God, that privation of being which is the origin of sin and despair; and unless the vision of nature as the ultimate value is informed by an intuition that takes it beyond its limitations, the naturist may easily fall a prey to the oppressive element of suffering. It is always easy for him to succumb to the mood of *A Shropshire Lad*:

> Now hollow fires burn out to black,
> And lights are guttering low:
> Square your shoulders, lift your pack,
> And leave your friends and go.
>
> Oh never fear, man, nought's to dread,
> Look not left nor right:
> In all the endless road you tread
> There 's nothing but the night.

Hudson knew the mood expressed in these lines; but he never succumbed to it. The contemplation of the dark side of nature, of change and death, gave rise to sorrow, but never to pessimism. 'Sorrow and pessimism are, indeed, in a sense, opposite things,' said Chesterton, 'since sorrow is founded on the value of something, pessimism on the value of nothing.' Sorrow expresses the natural grief which a creature designed for ultimate happiness must feel in the passing of whatever is good and beautiful. Pessimism is rooted in neurosis, and in the sin of despair. It was because Hudson regarded nature as the ultimate value, because he loved life and saw in it glimpses of life eternal, that he could grieve so much at the sad harmonies and crude discords in the symphony of creation. The loss of friends moved him profoundly—'still in my ears rings the poignant thrill in his voice, on the last day I saw him alive in August,' wrote Edward Garnett. '"What! is she *dead*?" he exclaimed, staring at me, when I spoke of the death of a woman writer we both admired. And his eyes reflected all the "intolerable regret" for the "beautiful multitudinous life that has vanished" . . .'

The emotional power of the passages of grief in Hudson's work is increased by their comparative rarity. Like the strange sad notes we sometimes hear in the sparkling music of the warblers, these passages are, in some mysterious way, integrally interwoven into the serene pattern of his utterance. He could enter into the feelings of the pessimist without being influenced by the views of the pessimist—indeed, he carefully distinguished feeling from conviction in these matters. 'Doubtless we all possess the feeling in some degree—the sense of loneliness and desolation and dismay at the thought of an uninhabited world and of long periods when man was not,' he writes in *Afoot in England*. We all possess the *feeling*; but we do not give way to it, nor build our philosophy of life upon it. Hudson was too much engrossed in the richness and beauty of the inhabited world to be tormented by the significance of the empty and barren. His attitude to suffering was, on the whole, balanced and constructive; albeit there were certain exceptions (largely unconscious) which occurred mainly in the Romances, of which I shall speak later.

His sense of the abiding value of nature gave Hudson the power, which all genuinely devoted people have, of living fully in the present. The future, which so oppresses and fascinates modern man, played little part in his life and work. In an age when the literary man has usurped the function of the prophet, and, despising the past and rebelling against the present, lives only for the Brave New World to come, Hudson is concerned with the art of living, here and now. Even his one Utopian effort, *A Crystal Age*, has been regarded as a lesson on the impossibility of all Utopias. The power of living in the present proceeds from the awareness of an ultimate value that frees us from anxiety about the world and allows the full play of our faculties at every moment. The saints with their abiding sense of the presence of God lived fully in every moment; and the presence of nature similarly affected Hudson. Both the pessimist and the optimist despise the present because both are lacking in a proper sense of value. The pessimist is backward-looking: the optimist is forward-looking. The pessimist is usually an extreme introvert: he despairs of the future and is wounded by the present, and such happiness as he is capable of experiencing derives from the past. The optimist is more often an exaggerated extravert: he dreams of the future, and is willing, within the varying degrees of his power, to starve and neglect his family, or to plunge the world into a blood bath for the realization of his dreams. Pessimism is a denial and perversion of the truth: optimism is a violent exaggeration of a particular aspect of the truth.

Hudson was a realist, and his realism allowed him to see the pitiless aspect of nature in its true perspective. He did not take a tortured satisfaction in defying it, as did Housman; nor did he ignore it. He saw it steadily, and accepted it, as in this typical passage from *Idle Days in Patagonia*. He is speaking of the war with nature—'a beautiful wayward Undine, delighting you with her originality, and most lovable when she teases most; a being of extremes, always either in laughter or tears, a tyrant and a slave alternately . . .' Man must accept her in all her aspects. He delights in her, and is yet at her mercy. She thwarts him, and again and again he retaliates.

He will not be beaten by her: he slays her striped and spotted creatures; he dries up her marshes; he consumes her forests and prairies with fire, and her wild things perish in myriads; he covers her plains with herds of cattle, and waving fields of corn, and orchards of fruit-bearing trees. She hides her bitter wrath in her heart, secretly she goes out at dawn of day and blows her trumpet on the hills, summoning her innumerable children to her aid. She is hard-pressed and cries to her children that love her to come and deliver her. Nor are they slow to hear. From north and south, from east and west, they come in armies of creeping things and in clouds that darken the air. Mice and crickets swarm in the fields; a thousand insolent birds pull his scarecrows to pieces, and carry off the straw stuffing to build their nests; every green thing is devoured; the trees, stripped of their bark, stand like great white skeletons in the bare desolate fields, cracked and scorched by the pitiless sun. When he is in despair deliverance comes; famine falls on the mighty host of his enemies; they devour each other and perish utterly. Still he lives to lament his loss; to strive still, unsubdued and resolute. She, too, laments her lost children, which now, being dead, serve only to fertilize the soil and give fresh strength to her implacable enemy. And she, too, is unsubdued; she dries her tears and laughs again; she has found out a new weapon it will take him long to wrest from her hands. Out of many little humble plants she fashions the mighty noxious weeds; they spring up in his footsteps, following him everywhere, and possess his fields like parasites, sucking up their moisture and killing their fertility. Everywhere, as if by a miracle, is spread the mantle of rich, green, noisome leaves, and the corn is smothered in beautiful flowers that yield only bitter seed and poison fruit. He may cut them down in the morning, in the night-time they will grow again. With her beloved weeds she will wear out his spirit and break his heart; she will sit still at a distance and laugh while he grows weary of the hopeless struggle; and at last, when he is ready to faint, she will go forth once more and blow her trumpet on the hills and call her innumerable children to come and fall on and destroy him utterly.

Such passages as this reveal the sanity of Hudson's approach to nature. The distinctive quality is acceptence—an acceptance that pervades all his work, and overflows continually into a deep joy, a delight in nature in all her moods. For Hudson, man, though he may war with nature, is himself a part of nature, and when he fights her on her own ground takes part in a family feud. Total war is the result of industrialism. In that battle, nature's trumpet on the hills is drowned by the klaxon horn and the hooter; and both nature and man are destroyed utterly. Hudson called us back to the thrill and exaltation of the ancient family feud: he called us to a delight in every aspect of nature, hostile or friendly. His vision embraced the whole world, from 'the grandeur of the starry heavens' to the humble grasses of the wayside; but above all it was a vision of earth with all her multitudinous life, and of man united with earth, receiving, and giving back to her within the mirror of his own mind.

THE MAN

Knowledge of a man's personality and the circumstances of his life may sometimes help us to a fuller understanding of his work, providing the life and work are genuinely related. Where the work is of an abstract or formal nature, personal details can be a hindrance; but where, as so often in literature, the work is a direct expression of the personality, such details can help us a good deal. This is, I think, particularly true of so individual a writer as Hudson, whose personality and art were intimately connected. Much of the charm of his writing derives from the friendly relation he establishes between himself and the reader. In this he is completely the reverse of the ultra-romantic, who is so absorbed in his own self-revelation that he is never able to make any contact with the reader. Hudson is both intimate and reserved. He describes what he sees and gives his own personal reactions; but he never deliberately intrudes himself. As we saw in the previous chapter, true personality proceeds not from the assertion of self, but from the loss of self in something greater which reflects it back in a fuller and deeper integration. It follows, then, that although we get a fairly complete picture of Hudson from his writings, this picture derives more from his devotion to nature than from any deliberate self-revelation. Hence, apart from the autobiography, *Far Away and Long Ago*, which only takes us up to adolescence, and a few allusions scattered about among his other books, Hudson tells us very little about the circumstances of his life. For information on this head we must go to objective sources, such as the memoir by his great friend Morley Roberts (*W. H. Hudson : a Portrait*), and certain notes and sketches by other friends and acquaintances, from whence we shall be able to glean various aspects of his personality which, together with the facts of his life, may help us more fully to understand his vision and appreciate his work. On this material, therefore—the intimate yet oblique revelations of Hudson himself, together with objective facts and data and the personal impressions of his friends—I shall do my best to draw a brief sketch of his character, following it by an outline of his life and working within the framework of ascertainable fact with regard to time and place.

Roberts's friendship with Hudson began many years after the period at which the Autobiography ends. Hudson was thirty-nine when Roberts first met him, and only at the beginning of his literary career; but from that time to his death—with one break of a few years soon after they met—Roberts gives us a fairly sustained record of the main events of his uneventful life. His book is, before all else, an intimate record of personal friendship; hence it is inevitably rather one-sided. There was a considerable difference in the ages of the two men. Hudson was many years older than Roberts, and was far and away the stronger personality. In spite of their genuine intimacy, Roberts seems to have stood rather in awe of him—an attitude that seems at times to have annoyed and embarrassed Hudson. Another thing that makes Roberts's portrait rather one-sided (faithful though it is in external details) is his tendency to read many of his own views into his friend. When, on occasion, Hudson would abstractedly and sometimes irritably agree with Roberts on some point, he would put it down as though it were Hudson's own considered opinion. But one can hardly blame Roberts: we all tend to read ourselves into those we love, and it was more than easy in the case of so rich and varied a personality as Hudson. Roberts gives us the portrait of a man of great charm and kindliness, but, as he grew older, often dogmatic, moody, and garrulous. Unfortunately, the most intimate part of the book is also, from the angle of character, the most incomplete. It is a verbatim record of conversations, and was based on notes taken down in Hudson's old age, when he was nearly eighty and suffering from an advanced form of heart trouble.

The quality that most impressed his other great friend, Edward Garnett, was his insight and sensibility. 'I knew and loved him intimately as a friend,' he writes, 'and I never remember a moment of tiredness, of dullness, of disappointment in his company. From the well-springs of his mind rose fresh, limpid waters.' H. J. Massingham spoke of 'his numerous but agreeably salty prejudices' which went with a personality 'very gracious and affectionate, if melancholy and a little lacking in humour.' (Roberts writes of his humour and high cackle.) The chief qualities that emerge from Coulson Kernahan's impression of Hudson are courtesy and humility. He speaks of 'the almost chivalrous courtesy of his bearing' which 'was shown to one and all, but noticeably to every woman with whom he had occasion to speak . . .' Kernahan found him shy but not self-conscious. Behind 'his friendliness was a reserve which only an impertinent person would have attempted to penetrate.' Hilaire Belloc's main impression was of 'a very sincere and enthusiastic man.' F. M. Ford tells the story of a glorious tussle between Belloc and Hudson at the Mont Blanc restaurant in Soho on some point of Sussex topography in which Hudson was the victor.

So far, all these impressions have been by men. Two women, one of them probably Naomi Morley Roberts, the other, Louise Chandler Moulton, the American poetess, have recorded very different impressions. The first describes him as 'unreasonable, petulant, and "contradictious," erratic and often unaccountable,' and speaks of his sanity and arrogance and self-sufficiency. 'He often shows a boy's pleasure in teasing, and sometimes when he 's being very unreasonable and knows it he has a humorous twinkle that 's delightful.' But she also speaks of 'his essential bigness . . . and, although he conceals it with feminine perversity, his real deep kindness.' Again, it must be remembered that the writer knew Hudson only in the later years of his life. The chief impression made upon L. C. Moulton was his isolation of spirit. 'He struck me as such a lonely—almost tragically lonely—man! I suspect that for some reason his life is unhappy'—a curious judgment in view of his intense joy in life.

When to these different viewpoints of Hudson's character we add the testimony of his books, the judgment of Roberts seems to have the ring of truth: 'He possessed in calm and equal qualities all the great characteristics of mankind, and such a noble and just balance of faculties may, perhaps, justify him as heroic when compared with most.' Undoubtedly much of Roberts's judgment is vitiated by his curiously adolescent tendency to hero-worship; but for all that, his *Portrait* bears the stamp of integrity and should be read by all who wish to possess some insight into Hudson's character.

The Hudson we have so far been discussing is a man experienced at first hand by individuals who loved and admired him. But it is possible that a clearer picture may be gained through the eyes of one who did not know him, and whose historical perspective enables him to weigh up all these different viewpoints plus the evidence of his acts and work. I make no claim to be specially qualified for this task, and at best I can only give a very broad and imperfect judgment.

There seems to have been in Hudson an egocentric strain that was not so much pride (his devotion saved him from that) as a certain solitariness of spirit that is almost inseparable from the aesthetic, and particularly the naturist, outlook. It accounts for the touch of arrogance, irritability, and capriciousness that seems to have disconcerted some of his friends at times. Again, like all men of deep sensibility, his mind was subject to the strain that goes with excessive activity of the imagination. But his character as a whole is not easily grasped. He was full of paradox.

He was the most conventional of men; and the most unconventional. His conservatism was like the conservatism of nature—a framework within which she is able to squander her fecund creativity. Within the unalterable tradition of seasonal change, day and night, birth, growth, and death, she hides a capricious spirit. In much the same way Hudson's conventionality and conservatism were the stabilizing factors that held in check the exuberant originality of his imagination. Out of the eyes of this reserved, conventional man there looked a half-wild and wholly inexplicable being who, to those who knew him intimately, would sometimes reveal strange aspects of himself. The rather humourless man would suddenly cackle wildly at some absurdity: the modest gentleman explode in a burst of arrogance: the conservative sweep away the whole world and all its institutions with a gesture.

He was born on the fourth of August 1841 in a house called 'The Twenty-five Ombú Trees,' ten miles outside Buenos Aires. Three strains united in him: English, Irish, and American. His paternal grandfather was a Devon man: his maternal grandmother was Irish. But his father and mother were both American born, his mother with American blood and tradition. I think there is no doubt that the English strain was predominant in Hudson. Certainly it was the origin of his conservatism. Whether he inherited anything of the American national character (a thing difficult to define) is doubtful, although along with his environment, America may have given him his sense of spacious freedom; but there is no doubt that the Celt in him—deeply hidden though it was—came out in his whimsicality and imaginative power. The persistence of the Irish strain is remarkable; and I have heard of characteristically Irish types whose sole connection with Ireland was through a single great-grandparent.

Hudson's environment in childhood and early youth seems to have been singularly fortunate. In the Autobiography we get a delightful picture of affectionate and carefree family life in the big rambling house on the Argentine pampas. The pampas, with their limitless horizons and rich, abundant wild life—above all the birds of many strange colours and shapes, great birds and small, solitary, and in immense flocks—were a perpetual inspiration. The character of Hudson's parents was no less an inspiration. His father was an exceptionally amiable and good-natured man, fearless almost to the point of folly. His mother was gentle, understanding, and dignified—at least, that is how he saw her, looking back over fifty years—and his devotion to her shines out from the final pages of the Autobiography. There is no doubt that, far more than heredity, the effect of environment is decisive. Modern psychology supports common sense in this matter. Hudson's heredity endowed him with a certain capacity and disposition; but his capacity was directed and his disposition developed by the happy effect of his surroundings and his parents.

He seems to have been quite an average child, not markedly different from his brothers and sisters except in his feeling for nature. But with the transition of childhood into adolescence he developed a solitary tendency that for a time alarmed his mother until she realized that it was due less to introspection than to intense observation. Later his life was complicated by religious problems and darkened by the fear of death, a fear increased by the dangerous illness which permanently injured his heart. Soon afterwards these problems were rendered acute by the impact of the new doctrine of evolution of which I have spoken earlier. His elder brother, returned from abroad, gave him a copy of *The Origin of Species*. Of its effect he has left us two separate and seemingly contradictory accounts. In *The Book of a Naturalist* he tells us that when, after he had read it, his brother asked for his opinion, '"It 's false!" I exclaimed in a passion . . .' But in the Autobiography he writes: 'When I had read and returned the book, and he was eager to have my opinion, I said that it had not hurt me in the least . . .' Now Hudson possessed a remarkable memory, and when we take into account the impact that Darwin's work must have made upon his sensitive, youthful mind, together with the fact that the two books quoted from above were separated from each other by only a year, it is exceedingly difficult to account for the contradiction. We must, however, remember that Hudson never really solved, but only shelved, the religious problem; hence I think it probable that this confusion of memory was due partly to disturbing psychological causes, and that the first account is probably the correct one, while the second represents what he would have liked to say, but failed on account of losing his temper. But we shall never know for certain. What we do know is that he was greatly affected by the book, and later read it again with deepening conviction.

The Autobiography closes soon after this incident, and with it ended Hudson's youth. Of the next fifteen years, until he came to England at the age of twenty-nine, little is known. He seldom spoke of it, even to his nearest friends. All we know is that during this period his parents died and the family dispersed, and he wandered about the country for some years. How he earned his living—unless by farming of some light sort (his health made heavy work impossible)—we do not know. But always England called him; and when at last he left South America it was to be for ever.

The first thing that struck him on arrival at Southampton was what he called 'the smell of England.' For some days he was greatly puzzled about this, until he discovered it to be hops! But if roasting hops was 'the smell of England' it was soon forgotten in the glory of the sights and sounds of the English countryside. Hudson loved the English countryside from his first sight of it, and loved it increasingly all his life. Those who, like him, have English traditions, but are born and reared in a foreign land, often possess a deeper love of England than the native.

They are, in a sense, exiles, and exile has increased their devotion. Hudson felt, when he stepped on to the shores of England, that he had come home; and it was in England—through his contact with the English literary tradition and the English landscape—that his genius flowered.

Yet his range of affection for England was circumscribed. Doubtless because he lived in London, he knew and loved best the home counties. Later he came to know the east coast and parts of the west country. But it was only after much persuasion from Roberts that he could be induced to visit Cornwall. When he did finally go there it became a favourite place to be revisited continually till the end of his life. Of the north he seems to have known only parts of Derbyshire. As far as I am aware, there is no evidence that he was familiar with Wales or Scotland, and he is said to have visited Ireland only once. As for Europe, it did not enter into his consciousness at all. Apart from his wanderings in South America as a young man, which may or may not have been extensive, it would be incorrect to call Hudson, as Frank Swinnerton does in *The Georgian Literary Scene*, a traveller. In the section of his book headed 'Travellers,' Swinnerton classes Hudson with Cunninghame Graham; but there was not much in common between the conservative lover of the home counties and the socialist hidalgo.

As I have said, Hudson resided in London; but of his early days there almost as little is known as of the previous period in South America. He seems to have made a bare living at all sorts of odd jobs, including the dull and thankless task of looking up genealogies for Americans of English origin. It was during this period that he married Emily Wingrave—a slight, gentle little woman, twenty years older than himself. She was rather lacking in personality, but made up for it with a charming voice and considerable musical talent. According to some reports she was quite a well-known professional singer in her youth; but by the time she met Hudson her voice was going, and though she appears to have given occasional singing lessons, neither his writing nor her teaching brought them enough to live on. Eventually they drifted into running a boarding house in Leinster Square, Bayswater.

Hudson's relationship with Emily was conventional enough. He was evidently very fond of her, and when they were apart, wrote to her every day; yet it remains mysterious that such a man should have chosen her for his mate. Some writers have speculated on whether he had a 'grand passion' in those hidden years of early manhood on the pampas. F. M. Ford, with characteristic hyperbole, writes that there is 'no doubt and no reason for preserving secrecy as to the fact that Hudson had once, far away and long ago, nourished an intolerable passion for a being who had a beautiful voice and sang from the gleaming shadows of the green mansion of an *ombú*.' But Roberts, his intimate friend, was of another opinion. He did not deny the possibility of such an affair, but, he said, 'it is a question if it was in him to love any one woman with a great passion and thereby put himself in chains.' I would incline to agree with Roberts. Hudson's great passion was nature; and so complete an absorption, like that of the religious mystic, would leave little room for human passion. It is possible for anything conceived as an ultimate value—God, nature, man, art—so to take possession of the entire man that passion dies out altogether. Most of the saints and many great artists and political leaders have been passionless and even sexless men. Whether, as a result of the sublimation of his senses in nature, passion—at least in the sense of sexual passion—died out of Hudson's life, or whether it had never developed, or whether it was there, but held in check, we cannot say; nor is it of much interest either way. But I recall a remark of Roberts to the effect that Mrs. Hudson sometimes made him think of Carlyle's wife.

Marriage with Emily seems to have given him contentment of a kind, and at first the boarding house brought them in a small but sufficient income. It was about this time that Hudson began to write his first books. But he met with no success. According to Coulson Kernahan, 'his first book, *The Purple Land that England Lost*, had aroused no interest among the reviewers, and was such a failure that Sampson Low and Marston, the publishers, "remaindered" at a heavy loss the greater part of the copies.' With the failure of the book went the failure of the boarding house, and the Hudsons were reduced to a condition very near starvation. 'One week we lived on a tin of cocoa and milk,' he told Roberts. Nobody seemed in the least interested in his books and articles. 'I almost went down on my knees and begged publishers to take my work.' It is difficult to know what fate would have befallen them if Emily had not suddenly come into a property in St. Luke's Road, Bayswater, about a mile away from Leinster Square—a large, conventional house which they let off into flats, retaining a couple of rooms for themselves. Here they lived for over thirty years; and here Hudson died. The rents kept them just solvent, and when an occasional cheque for an article or singing lessons arrived, they packed up and went roaming the countryside together. Often Hudson went alone, and as Emily grew older she could no longer be 'the companion of his walks.'

It is impossible to conceive of any greater incongruity than this naturist visionary cooped up in such a place as No. 40, St. Luke's Road, Bayswater. It is not too bad a place as suburban houses go—I know it well, and used to pass it every day at one time, and have been inside; but for Hudson it must have been a cage. The mystery is why he chose to live there when he could have lived where he liked. In the later years of his life he had a Civil List pension which, together with the sale of his books—especially *Green Mansions* in America—brought him in a small but steady income; and the house at Bayswater could have been sold for quite a reasonable sum. But perhaps Emily clung to her property as women will, and by the time she died Hudson was too old to bother about selling, and had come to take the place for granted.

I have sometimes thought that London may have been for Hudson a compensation for the loneliness of spirit which derives from communion with nature, and that its vast and teeming life provided the human side he might otherwise have lacked. Or he may have seen in London, with its incredible vitality and diversity, not a city built with human hands, but a huge forest of stone grown out of the earth. A love of London is not incompatible with the naturist outlook, as witness Jefferies who, though far more extreme in his naturism than Hudson, had a genuine affection for London which, he said, was 'the only *real* place in the world.' Hudson was able to extract enjoyment out of the most trivial incident, as in the Cockney story he often recounted to Roberts with immense gusto. A man and his wife were quarrelling in a shabby street when suddenly the man turned to the bystanders, among whom Hudson was quietly standing, and said in an impassioned tone: 'Now what I want to know is this: Is a man a king in his own castle or is he an antediluvian?' Hudson visited the cinema, and got enormous fun out of Charlie Chaplin in *A Dog's Life*. But whether observing some absurdity in the street, or paying his shilling to see Chaplin, or lunching with the Galsworthys or with Roberts at Whiteley's, or visiting the literary clique at the 'Mont Blanc,' Hudson managed to extract a good deal of interest and enjoyment out of London. Yet there was one side of him that hated all cities. 'I have lived in these colonies years and years,' he wrote, 'never losing the sense of captivity, of exile, ever conscious of my burden, taking no interest in the dealings of that innumerable multitude.' Obviously this passage was dictated by mood; for why should he lament his exile when he could have packed up and left London for good and all whenever he liked? Perhaps he was like the Chinaman in Thomas Burke's story who worked in London but was for ever dreaming of China, and when at last some kind people secretly got up a subscription for his fare home, he hanged himself in his deep despair at having to leave the London he loved. However we look at it, Hudson's sojourn in one of the dullest suburbs in London for over thirty years remains a mystery. Perhaps his vision of earth glowed more brightly on the inward eye in such incongruous surroundings, for he wrote much of his best work at St. Luke's Road. But we shall never know with any certainty what held him.

It can be argued that Hudson did not choose St. Luke's Road: it was thrust upon him. But in Penzance, where he wintered during the last years of his life, he deliberately selected apartments in a dull street right inside the town. Roberts exaggerated the dreariness of North Parade; but it was an extraordinary place for such a man to choose as his permanent winter address, above all, in view of the fact that in the early days before he knew Cornwall, he had written to Roberts from Penzance, 'To stay in this squalid place is impossible.' St. Luke's Road in summer, and North Parade in winter! And yet it was in these two incongruous places that he wrote his inspired masterpiece, *A Hind in Richmond Park*. But, as I have said, he was full of paradox; and the last paradox of his life was that death should have come to him at St. Luke's Road. Somewhere in one of his books, Osbert Sitwell makes one of his characters comment on the fitting cirucmstances of the deaths of certain great men such as Shelley and Edgar Allan Poe. But Hudson's death was supremely unfitting. He who loved the wind on the heath and the sound of wings, died in a first-floor bed-sitting-room at Bayswater. It was high summer; and far away from the heat and dust of London, nature was busy with her multitudinous life.

Hudson died on the eighteenth of August 1922; and on the day after, Edward Garnett looked upon him for the last time. 'I saw,' he writes, 'the calm death-mask of a strong chieftain. All the chiselled, wavy lines of his wide brow, the brooding mournfulness and glowing fire of his face had been smoothed out. He was lying like some old chief of the Bronze Age, who, through long years of good and ill, had led his tribe. And now for him only remained the ancient rites, the purging fire, the cairn on the hillside and the eternity of the stars, the wind, the sun.' But he was buried with Emily at Worthing.

Our bewilderment at the paradoxes of his life would have amused him; for I think that he delighted in his own strangeness as he did in the strangeness of others. Without paradox there can be no character. Consistency, admirable up to a point, kills the vital tensions generated by paradox within which character develops. According to Roberts Hudson was 'bigger than his books'— and if by this he meant that any human soul is worth more than any book he was uttering an obvious truism. But if he meant that the Hudson sketched above was greater than the man who spoke in his works, he was mistaken. The work is greater than the man, for it is that in him which partakes of the eternal.

THE WORK

THE ROMANCES

'HUDSON writes as the grass grows.' The saying, attributed to Conrad, is often quoted; but it happens to be untrue. Hudson's best work certainly gives the impression of having been written 'as the grass grows,' though, in point of fact, it was the result of a highly self-conscious and deliberate art. According to Roberts, he seldom wrote more than a few hundred words daily, and F. M. Ford has told us how he 'would sweat over correcting and re-correcting his work.' Very little is known of his actual methods on account of his reticence and passion for destroying manuscripts and letters. Ford mentions a change from 'the hedges grew green' to 'the hedges were green' as typical. Always he sought for the clearest expression of his art. In one of his books he speaks disparagingly of writers who are always in a hurry and do poor work on that account. Hudson never hurried; and fortunately he had the leisure in which to write when and where he chose, and to correct slowly at his ease. To have a settled income, however small and from whatever source—even though derived from a tenement house in Bayswater—is a great advantage to a writer. The full-time professional, when he is not slogging at journalism, often tends to think overmuch of his public and as a result works too eagerly and too fast.

The care, spaciousness, and leisure of Hudson's approach to his art is evident in all he wrote—even in his poorest work. His style is very satisfying; but it is by no means easy to analyse. It is not a 'perfect' style in the academic sense. I would describe it as natural and easy, not without a certain colloquial touch, but always musical and masculine, and adapted to the expression of very varied emotions. In essence it is what all good style should be, individual without being peculiar. Although the majority of his books are written in the first person, his individuality is never obtrusive.

We shall perhaps understand something more of the secret of Hudson's style if we consider the influence behind it. He was bilingual in youth, reading widely in both English and Spanish, and the felicitous blend of the two languages—the imaginative power of English and the rhythm and music of Spanish—is very obvious in his best work. The Spanish influence is predominant in the Romances (which are, with one exception, set in South America) and the English influence in the Essays. Two friends of mine, an old couple who had spent a great part of their lives in the Argentine and were not at all 'literary,' at once drew attention to the Spanish style of Hudson's early Romance, *The Purple Land*, when I lent it to them.

The Romances, which are mainly of Hudson's earlier period, have a curiously artificial quality at times, and are laboured by contrast with the Essays. I find it difficult to discover any completely satisfying explanation for this, but there are several possible reasons. It may be that fiction was not altogether congenial to Hudson; or perhaps the fault was immaturity. But if the fault was immaturity, it is strange that the Essays written about this time are relatively free from it. I have sometimes thought that the artificial quality of the Romances may have been due to the effect of writing imaginatively about South America with its Spanish associations, which caused him to think in Spanish while writing in English; but this explanation is not very adequate.

Perhaps the true explanation resides in Hudson's character. The Romances and Essays are both in the first person; but whereas the narrator of the Romances is fictitious, the narrator of the Essays is real. Now it seems to me that a writer would not consistently employ the first person unless he desired to express some aspect of himself, and we may reasonably assume that the narrator of the Romances is, to some extent, Hudson. In the previous chapter I alluded to certain inconsistencies in his character, and it is possible that in the Romances he gave vent imaginatively to those elements in him which he normally suppressed, and which only emerged occasionally in everyday life. But integration was destroyed in the process, with the result that the narrator of the Romances is unreal. The man who emerges from the Essays, the observing field naturalist, sensitive, compassionate, charming, very sane, and rather conventional, may not be the whole Hudson; but he is convincing. The narrator of the Romances, a queer composite—primitive, emotional, passionate, cynical, pessimistic, self-absorbed—does not ring true either in himself or in the sentiments he expresses. The narrator of the Romances is a fantasy self: hence his artificiality; for only the self built up in accordance with the highest part of a man, his rational nature operating through continual efforts of the will, is genuine. The fantasy self, whether moral or immoral, is bogus; and the attempt to express it imaginatively leads to strain, with the resultant artificial effect. We see this in the case of Dickens, who, in spite of his many virtues, was far more like his bad and eccentric than his good characters—which explains why his bad and eccentric characters ring true, while the virtuous creations of his fantasy self are unconvincing. Hudson's case was the reverse. His conventional naturalist was real: his erotic adventurers were false. The unconventional narrator of the Romances is conventional and artificial: the conventional narrator of the Essays is unique.

The erotic element is, to me, the weakest part of the Romances. It is true that the description and analysis of erotic emotion is a pitfall for the majority of authors; but Hudson's efforts in this direction seem to me quite extraordinarily unconvincing. Whether or no he ever experienced the grand passion spoken of by Ford, the love scenes in the Romances—the cynical dallying of Lamb in *The Purple Land*, the sentimental amorousness of Smith in *A Crystal Age*, or the half-crazed passion of Abel in *Green Mansions*—appear to be the work of a man who had experienced none of these things. He who was so great a stylist becomes awkward and stilted, and at times almost absurd, when he attempts to write the language of erotic love.

In the field of general characterization and description the Romances are more successful—though Hudson could hardly be called a great and vivid creator of character. His characters, though unusual, are never wholly convincing. In the Essays he could bring an old English shepherd or a South American gaucho before us vividly and truthfully in a sentence. He could do the same with animals and birds. He created more effectively when he was re-creating as a field naturalist than when he was inventing as a novelist. Even in the realm of description, even though some of the nature passages in *A Crystal Age* and *Green Mansions* are of high inspiration, there is nowhere the sustained evocation of the presence of nature that we find in the Essays. I think Hudson was probably aware that fiction was not his true medium, since he used the form very rarely, and then mostly in his earlier period. But the fact that he used it at all seems to indicate that he felt the need to express something within him, normally hidden, even from himself.

Hudson's plots, in the longer Romances at any rate, are weak and laboured, and he gets his best effects from vivid incidents within the plot. There is, however, one distinguishing note that gives to the Romances their significance and justification: the note of tragedy. Apart from one or two short stories and *The Purple Land*, all the books usually grouped as Romances might just as well be called Tragedies. I am not suggesting that tragedy is their only justification. I mean that tragedy is their supreme merit, and sets them apart from the Essays on a pedestal of their own. There are people who find Thomas Hardy a rather commonplace story-teller, but justify him by his sense of tragedy—a quality that imparts grandeur to his books as a whole, in spite of the weaknesses of particular sections. The same may be said of Hudson as a novelist. But his sense of tragedy was not rooted in the conscious pessimism of Hardy: it proceeded from an unconscious struggle. His naturistic creed impressed upon him the continual presence of change and death and loss; and, though sublimated in his conscious every-day life and controlled in its expression in the Essays, his rebellion against these forces erupted at times when a momentary flash of disillusionment, a sudden vivid perception of the emptiness of nature divorced from a living personal God came to him. This emotion did not harmonize with his conscious affirmative attitude to life. It was suppressed, emerging in the tragic fantasy of the Romances.

When considering the difference between pessimism and sorrow, and the strain of sadness in Hudson's outlook earlier on, I said that I should have to qualify some of my statements when dealing with the Romances; and undoubtedly these stories do represent, to some extent, a darker side of his nature than elsewhere. But the dark emotion, though existing largely below the level of consciousness, was genuine, and there was nothing laboured or artificial in the tragic situations of the Romances. In these tales Hudson gave full expression to the sense of pity that, according to Aristotle, is one of the main ingredients of tragedy. The effect of tragedy, the philosopher tells us, is to arouse emotions of pity and fear in the audience (and it follows that the author of tragedy must himself have experienced these emotions if his work is to have any element of greatness), who are purified of their own excess of pity and fear and project it on to the situations of the tragedy. In the words of Lascelles Abercrombie, 'in so far as the emotions roused by the spectacle of the evil in life—not merely moral evil, but the evil of destruction and waste and misfortune—are by tragedy deprived of evil effect, and even made beneficial, something like "purification" may be alleged.' He adds that 'by reason of the unity of tragic drama, even the misfortune of life becomes an instance of the world we most profoundly desire. This accounts for the peculiar pleasure we take in tragedy. Things which in real life would be merely distressing become in tragedy nobly exhilarating. They do not cease to be distressing; but something is added to this; whereby their evil becomes our good.' In this connection it seems that we gain some illumination on the age-old problem of God's eternal perfection and happiness and His awareness of man's sorrow and suffering. The effect of our evil (not the evil itself, which is negation) becomes His good.

Tragedy, as thus defined, is a noble thing. But the tragedy of the atheist-pessimist is not of this kind. It derives from the rejection of God who, though not consciously believed to exist, still gives the standard of lost perfection. Such men cannot accept the universe simply as unexplained brute fact; nor do they seem to realize that the lost standard of perfection with which they contrast the evil futility of the world tacitly implies the God whom they reject. They see that there ought to be ultimate justice, but refuse to accept the only ground for justice. As Kant, and also Robespierre, saw, our sense of justice in an unjust universe demands ultimate justice in God. The aesthetic reaction to the denial of God gives rise to what I would call *cosmic* tragedy. Human tragedy is not the same thing: it arises not from ultimate negativity, but from human nature—partly from the limitations of ideas, partly, as Hegel saw, from the conflict of different aspects of the good, and partly from the folly and wickedness of individuals. On the whole, the best of the classical tradition of tragedy was of this human kind. But cosmic tragedy is centred in the conflict of man's aspirations with a pitiless impersonal reality. It never rings true; and it lacks both the dignity and power of human tragedy. Hudson's Romances have in them something of both kinds of tragedy, though the human note is predominant. There are elements of cosmic tragedy; but nature was, for him, the ultimate *value*, and included man as its summit; hence the sense of value redeems the cosmic tragedy implicit in his outlook, and throws into relief the human element. We may say that Hudson's feeling for tragedy was, in the true classical manner, human, and that the rare but disquieting note of cosmic tragedy proceeded from his doubt as to the survival of the soul after death. At the deepest levels of his intuition he saw that if the individual does not survive, our sense of justice is a mockery, and the world at best a terrifying riddle. The believer in personal immortality is often criticized for what is called his selfish desire for survival; but the criticism is superficial. Belief in immortality derives from the sense of justice; and I find it difficult to imagine the state of mind of one who can affirm that the hideous life of a man, tortured and murdered in a concentration camp in the flower of his youth, and the easy life of a cultured hedonist who dies at a ripe old age, are each final and complete. Hudson saw the force of such arguments. He doubted and suffered, and put the doubt away from him. But he never solved the problem; and from time to time it passed across his mind like a dark cloud. It is essential to bear this in mind always in reading the Romances. Consciously, as we have seen, Hudson accepted life joyously; but the Romances contain elements that represent the forces of his unconscious, his conflicts and his doubts.

An important aspect of tragedy, sometimes overlooked, is irony. Like tragedy, irony can be cosmic or human according to the angle of approach. The first exhibits man as the puppet of impersonal forces: the second derives primarily from the culpability of man. The nature of both kinds of irony has been admirably defined by Belloc.

Concerning what I have called cosmic irony he writes: 'There is irony when, every defence having been made against some natural accident, that accident yet enters by another gate unsuspected to man.' And elsewhere he describes irony (that is, what I mean in the sense of human irony) as that which 'should avenge the truth.' Hudson's irony is mainly human, and is directed towards avenging the truth that man can only default from nature at his peril. Most of the misfortunes of his characters proceed from some human wickedness, weakness, or folly; but nature, even in her most wayward moods, is always the great healer, the bringer of refreshment and peace. For Hudson, man's suffering is largely due to his rejection of nature.

To sum up the Romances as a whole, before passing on to a more detailed treatment, I would say that, in spite of the weakness of the erotic situations, the characterization, and to some extent, the plot and construction, they are redeemed by fantasy, tragedy, and irony. This curious interaction of weakness and power, artificiality and inspiration, makes them formally unsatisfying; yet at their best they make an unforgettable impression, and take us into a strange and haunting world of the imagination.

As we have seen, Hudson's published fiction represents a comparatively small part of his output. If we exclude the early and uncharacteristic novel *Fan: the Story of a Young Girl's Life*, published under the pseudonym Henry Harford, and *Ralph Herne*, which appeared serially in the magazine *Youth*, the rest of his fiction comprises only three complete novels and a group of long short stories.

The first of the Romances, *The Purple Land*, was also Hudson's first published book; and for a first book it is a remarkable achievement. This is not difficult to understand. He was past middle life and intellectually mature, and for many years had observed keenly and thought deeply. He had also made a large number of notes from a wide, varied, and unusual experience. Intellectually and emotionally the harvest was ready; but he lacked the practice of his art. It is possible that he had been writing for some time—indeed, he must have had some experience to have produced *The Purple Land*; nevertheless, remarkable though it is, the book is stylistically immature. The Spanish influence is very evident in the rhythm, and there is often an indefinable quality of uncertainty in the syntax.

The Purple Land concerns the travels of Richard Lamb in the Banda Orientál. The plot—if one can call it that—is slender, and the book is really a series of adventures linked together by the personality of the narrator, Lamb, who has the doubtful distinction of being amorous and selfish. But he is not a live figure. The love scenes are rather stilted and, at times, irritatingly artificial. The book is notable chiefly for its humour and intensely human irony. All the adventures (or misfortunes) of the characters have in them something of the grotesque and absurd. Hudson's weakness in characterization is less noticeable in this book than elsewhere, since he knew the gaucho mentality intimately, and could enter into and sympathize with it. They are a primitive and childlike people with a streak of cruelty which, though partly buried in normal times, comes out during social differences and in war. *The Purple Land* is, to some extent, drawn from life; and it is probably because Hudson is re-creating and reliving his characters (a process at which his genius was supreme), rather than directly inventing, that his characterization is more successful than in some of the other Romances. It is far from being a vintage Hudson, but is worth reading for its incidents and stories, some of which, taken singly, are admirable. The soliloquies at the beginning and end are among the best things in the book, and contain impressive passages having something of the power of the later Hudson.

Some who, knowing no other Hudson, have come upon *The Purple Land* for the first time have expressed astonishment at the insignificant part played in it by nature. They have heard of Hudson as a naturalist, and find only a travel book about love among the gauchos. But apart from the fact that at this period Hudson was badly in need of money and would not have stood much chance with publishers if he had written about animals and birds, we must remember that, for him, nature included human nature, and human nature was very close to the wild in the South America of the last century. If once we realize this we shall not hesitate to class *The Purple Land* as a nature book. Over it all, and over everything he wrote, was the spirit of nature—the sense of mystery and of great spaces.

For a first book, *The Purple Land* was unusual; but Hudson's next Romance, *A Crystal Age*, though full of the characteristic faults of his fiction, was absolutely original and could have come from no other pen. I have discussed some aspects of it earlier and shall not say much more here. It tells of the projection into the future of Smith, a young man of our time, and of the strange pastoral people he discovers. They are deeply human and affectionate, and live in small communities housed in buildings of great beauty. Each community is presided over by the Father and replenished by the Mother; and the members pass their time in a mixture of aesthetic contemplation and enjoyment, and vigorous open-air life. Smith is accepted as a guest in one of the communities, and falls in love with Yoletta, a young and beautiful girl whom we may regard as a sketch for the later and more satisfying figure of Rima. But in the end, through drinking a forbidden potion, Smith loses Yoletta and the Crystal Age for ever. The note of human tragedy, of the never-never land, of exile and loss due to the folly and greed of modern man typified by Smith pervades the book, and along with the descriptions of nature, justifies it to some extent. But it lacks substance; and the love scenes and the Mother episodes are laboured and far too prolonged.

Roberts thought little of *A Crystal Age*, and tells us that

Hudson himself 'looked back upon its pages without satisfaction'; but Belloc had a high opinion of it. It is, he wrote, 'the most complete expression that I know of the Unknown Country.' This atmosphere of an Unknown Country pervades all Hudson's work. The humblest places take on an original character. He will describe a village in Sussex, well known to the reader, who sees it suddenly with a shock, as something familiar yet strange; and in that moment he has glimpsed the Unknown Country. But I doubt if this quality of 'otherness' is increased in *A Crystal Age*: rather, the effort to create a Utopia that is, in any case, doomed, seems to have inhibited Hudson's deepest inspiration.

A Crystal Age was followed, some years later, by the long short story entitled *El Ombú* which, many years afterwards, was included, with other short stories, in a single volume. The stories are rather unequal; but two, *El Ombú* itself, and *Marta Riquelme*, are outstanding in Hudson's fiction, the latter being one of the greatest things he ever wrote.

In my opinion, Hudson's work in the sphere of fiction was best suited to the short story form. There are writers, such as Tolstoy and Dickens, who express themselves best in the long and involved story, and who think in terms of plots that carry the weight of such length. Hudson, on the other hand, seemed to think in terms of plots that are essentially terse, vivid, and compelling; and this, while it obliged him to spin out unduly the material of the longer novels, made for success in the short story. Again we must remember that Hudson was primarily an essayist; and an essayist is one who tends to think in isolated incidents, even when they are interwoven so as to form a unified whole. As a naturalist, the essay suited Hudson perfectly—in fact, many of his essays contain what are best described as short stories 'from the life.' Conrad asserted that the long short story was the ideal form in fiction. It is certainly an underrated form, and in the hands of a master such as Hudson can be supremely satisfying. Most books are far too long, and I believe that literature would benefit considerably if authors reduced many of their novels to the length of *Marta Riquelme* and their ideological writings to the compass of Descartes's *Discourse* and Rousseau's *Social Contract*.

El Ombú and *Marta Riquelme* are perfect examples of the long short story. Tragedy of the most stark and terrible kind dominates them. The narrative in each case is concentrated and vivid, and nowhere else has Hudson shown so much intensity of feeling. Although there are crudities and occasional lapses into artificiality, the inspiration is of such a high quality that these faults are reduced to insignificance, and even, in places, transformed into their own justification. The artificial becomes the grotesque. We are borne along in a torrent of inspiration in which faults are either swept aside and lost, or else merge with the torrent, flashing and darkening as it goes on its way. Such crudities as exist only serve to heighten the grotesqueness that characterizes the two stories. There is a note of madness in them. In each, the erotic element is subordinate, and Hudson avoids the irritating 'stage' amorousness of so many of his fictitious lovers. He is able to do this partly on account of the form of the stories. *El Ombú* is related by an old man and only concerns him indirectly, and the narrator of *Marta Riquelme*, though active in the story, is a Jesuit priest. The love of which *El Ombú* tells is hopeless and lost from the start; and in *Marta Riquelme*, although the narrator is deeply in love with the central figure, his love is unexpressed, unconsummated, and hardly distinguishable from pity.

The story of *El Ombú* is told beneath an ombú-tree 'in the shade, one summer's day, by Nicandro, that old man to whom we all loved to listen.' The plot, which is too involved to be given here, concerns the inhabitants of a house that long ago stood under the shade of the tree, and of which nothing now remains but a bed of nettles. 'They say that sorrow and at last ruin comes upon the house on whose roof the shadow of the ombú-tree falls; and on that house which now is not, the shadow of this tree came every summer day when the sun was low.' The note of doom is sounded from the first, and the dreadful catalogue of frustrated love and cruelty moves forward inexorably. One of the most frightful incidents in all Hudson's imaginative writing occurs in this book. The sadistic General Barboza is suffering from some obscure kind of blood poisoning, and an old soldier famous for his cures suggests that he should be dipped into the warm blood of a newly killed bull. He agrees to submit to this treatment. The bull is killed and the men stand round, many 'prepared to greet the reappearance of the General with a loud cheer.' But he emerges naked and streaming red from that terrible bath with a sword in his hand, shouting, raving mad. Occasionally the narrative lapses into something very like melodrama; but it is always compelling, and the tragedy is broken by passages of rare beauty, as in the incident of the death of Valerio. After terrible undeserved sufferings and hardships, Valerio, 'so brave, so generous even in his poverty, of so noble a spirit, yet so gentle,' returns home to his wife, Donata, only to fall dead of exhaustion before the door of the house. Every day afterwards, Donata pours water on the place where he fell. It was hard and dry, trodden by the feet of countless men and horses, and baked by the sun; but 'after a long time of watering a little green began to appear in the one spot; and the green was of a creeping plant with small round malava-like leaves, and little white flowers like porcelain shirt-buttons.' The story closes on a note of peace. Monica—the lover of Bruno, son of Valerio—now grown old and having lost her reason through the cruel death of Bruno, finds consolation at last in nature:

To see her you would hardly believe that she is the Monica I have told you of, whom I knew as a little one, running barefooted after her father's flock. For she has grey hairs and wrinkles now. As you ride to Chascomus from this point you will see, on approaching the lake, a very high bank on your left hand, covered with a growth of tall fennel, hoarhound, and cardoon thistle. There on most days you will find her, sitting on the bank in the shade of the tall fennel bushes, looking across the water. She watches for the flamingoes. There were many of those great birds on the lake, and they go in flocks, and when they rise and travel across the water, flying low, their scarlet wings may be seen at a great distance. And every time she catches sight of a flock moving like a red line across the lake she cries out with delight. That is her one happiness—her life. And she is the last of all those who have lived in my time at El Ombú.

Of *Marta Riquelme* Roberts tells us that Hudson himself rated it the best of his stories. 'Assuredly it was Hudson's opinion, often declared to me, that the one story he looked on as his best was . . . the mournful and dreadful tale of the imagination, "Marta Riquelme."' As a rule, authors are notoriously wrong in their judgments of their own work; but Hudson appears to have been an exception. His opinions of *A Crystal Age* and of *Marta Riquelme* seem to me absolutely right. *Marta* is unique among his writings for sustained intensity of feeling. The narrative is fierce, ruthless, terrifying. It tells of the Kakué fowl, a bird into which men and women who have endured great and prolonged suffering are believed to be changed, and of Marta, a gentle-natured and beautiful woman who, after unimaginable sufferings, at last, at the height of her agony and degradation, vanishes, leaving behind her the ill-omened bird. The narrator—a virtuous, imaginative, but rather intellectually-limited Jesuit priest who loves Marta and is full of pity for her—is drawn with insight and sympathy. Although occasionally Hudson allows himself to be ironical at the expense of beliefs he does not accept, on the whole he tries to understand. The narrator of *Marta Riquelme* is far more convincing than the other selves Hudson assumes elsewhere in his fiction. There is still a certain amount of artificiality and strain—it is never entirely absent from the Romances—but, probably because the narrator was so remote from any aspect of Hudson's character, he succeeds in imparting to him a genuine and integral characterization.

The story opens ominously. The priest is resting under the shade of a great tree, when suddenly, from the depths of the leafage above, he hears 'a shriek, the most terrible it has ever fallen to the lot of any human being to hear.' It is repeated again and again, and he is unable to discover the cause. Later, a man to whom he recounts his experience, tells him that it is the Kakué fowl, and acquaints him with the legend. The story goes on to tell of Marta, and of the dreadful calamities that befall her. She is captured by Indians and sold as wife to a native, and her child is taken from her. At length she returns; but her husband renounces her because of her repulsive appearance, due to the cruel treatment of the Indians. After further terrible sufferings and privations, in her extremity she flees to a dense wood on a high inaccessible slope. The priest goes in search of her, and finds her at last seated on the trunk of a fallen tree 'which was sodden with the rain and half buried under great creepers and masses of dead and rotting foliage.' But her eyes 'were no longer those soft violet orbs which had retained until recently their sweet pathetic expression; now they were round and wild-looking, open to thrice their ordinary size, and filled with a lurid yellow fire, giving them a resemblance to the eyes of some hunted savage animal.' In his horror the priest holds his crucifix before her; but with wild despair she thrusts it aside. Her short hair 'rose up until it stood like an immense crest on her head . . . and presently flinging up her arms, she burst forth into shrieks so terrible in the depth of agony they expressed that overcome by the sound I sank upon the earth and hid my face.' When he looked up, Marta was gone. 'In another form—that strange form of the Kakué—she had fled out of our sight for ever to hide in those gloomy woods which were henceforth to be her dwelling place.' Hudson preserves credibility by leaving us free to assume that the sick and overwrought priest imagined Marta's transformation; but such is the power of the writing that the reader imagines it no less.

It will be observed from the above brief quotations that the language is baroque and highly charged; but the effect of the whole is so tremendous that exaggerations are overridden. The originality and power of this concentrated outpouring of genius sweeps away every defect. Hudson's Romances are not, on the whole, the best of his work; but *El Ombú* and *Marta Riquelme* are exceptions, and take their place among the great short stories of English fiction.

Green Mansions, the last full-length work of fiction to be written by Hudson, is considered by many critics to be his best. It is certainly the best of the long Romances, and makes its predecessors, *A Crystal Age* and *The Purple Land*, seem amateurish by comparison. But, in spite of its many virtues, it is an imperfect work. A great deal of it is inspired; and a great deal is manufactured. Hudson worked at it for many years and gave infinite pains to its composition, and if he failed to produce a work of art commensurate with his effort it was probably because, as I said earlier on, it did not represent a genuine experience. No one would deny the originality, strangeness, and tragic power of the book. But it is inferior to the best of the Essays.

For reasons not altogether easy to assess, *Green Mansions* became 'popular.' F. M. Ford speaks of the excellent sales in America during Hudson's lifetime. The royalties brought him many comforts in his old age, though he was never, in any sense of the expression, well off. The book is known to many who have read no other Hudson; and one will find among such casual readers some who dislike it intensely, and others whose enthusiasm is beyond description. But whatever the reaction may be, it always makes a profound impression. *Green Mansions* is a book one can never forget.

The story is narrated by Abel, a Venezuelan. Wanted, in his youth, for being vaguely mixed up in one of the interminable South American revolutionary plots, he flees the country, and penetrates into a little-known part of the hinterland of Venezuela, where he falls in with an Indian tribe. He decides to stay with them for a time, and later discovers, at some distance from the camp, a deserted forest which strangely attracts him. Wandering in the forest, he hears a marvellous warbling like the sound made by some ethereal being, half bird, half human. He inquires of the Indians concerning the voice, and they tell him that it is the Daughter of the Didi, a malign spirit of the forest of whom they are greatly afraid. At length he is rewarded by seeing the owner of the voice, not a malign spirit, but Rima, a young and beautiful girl, who lives in a clearing of the forest with Nufflo, her grandfather, and has become assimilated to the nature of the place and its wild inhabitants. Abel falls in love with Rima, but finds her elusive, and her heart set upon a journey to a far-distant place where once her mother dwelt. To please her they set out on the long journey, and at last Rima reveals her love for Abel. But the journey is fruitless. They decide to return, Rima first, alone, the grandfather and Abel following. When they reach the clearing in the forest they find the home burnt to the ground and Rima vanished. Sick at heart, Abel goes back to the Indians to discover news of Rima. He learns that they have burned her to death in a great tree in which she had taken shelter from them. He searches for the tree and finds it at last, gathering the remains of Rima's bones in his cloak. Nufflo has since been killed by the Indians, and after burying him, Abel, overwhelmed with grief and despair, and already half mad, builds a rough hut over the remains of the old home, and there sets to work to carve an urn for the reception of Rima's bones. At last, after a long period of sickness and delirium and insanity, he gets back to civilization, bringing the urn with him. That is a bare outline of the story.

Whether Hudson consciously intended it or not, we cannot help seeing in Rima the symbol of nature destroyed by the brutality of men. She is the ideal of nature—all that is highest and most abundantly alive in the world. She is what Hudson desired human nature to be.

Although the plot is of great beauty and originality, it is too slender and lacking in situation for a book of over three hundred pages. Hudson would, I think, have succeeded better (as I suggested earlier in relation to all his full-length novels) if he had cast it in the form of a long short story such as *El Ombú*. It may be that he was too much in love with it, and lingered unduly. But if this was the case, the attempt to make a full-length novel out of material best suited to the short story because of a personal feeling was not aesthetically justifiable and was bound to fail.

The artificiality and strain which is present in all the Romances is very evident in parts of *Green Mansions*, especially in those sections which are unduly prolonged. But the descriptions of nature are of a high inspiration and contain some of Hudson's most sensitive writing. The mystery and menacing beauty of the great South American forest is marvellously evoked. It impresses us with the reality of a first-hand experience—although according to his own testimony, Hudson was 'never in a forest.' But his feeling for nature and power of imagination were such that he was able to create what he had not directly experienced. Unfortunately he was less successful with the creation of human types. The characterization is weak, and the minor personalities such as Nufflo are negligible. When Hudson was re-creating from his direct experience—as in the case of the Indians—he was more successful. Old Clá-clá, the nurse, is unforgettable, and altogether the Indians are the most convincing people in the book. But the narrator is unconvincing, and the same must be said, to some extent, of Rima. Hudson attempted the impossible task of creating an ethereal being symbolic of nature who is, at the same time, a young girl of flesh and blood, beautiful and desirable. The result is that we are impressed with the general conception of Rima while being continually irritated by her detailed presentation.

The chapters leading up to her appearance are full of mystery and prescience. Wandering in the forest, Abel is attracted by the confused cries and calls of a multitude of birds.

After that tempest of motion and confused noises the silence of the forest seemed very profound; but before I had been resting many moments it was broken by a low strain of exquisite bird-melody, wonderfully pure and expressive, unlike any musical sound I had ever heard before. It seemed to issue from a thick cluster of broad leaves of a creeper only a few yards from where I sat. With my eyes fixed on this green hiding-place I waited with suspended breath for its repetition, wondering whether any civilized being had ever listened to such a strain before. Surely not, I thought, else the fame of so divine a melody would long ago have been noised abroad. I thought of the rialejo, the celebrated organ-bird or flute-bird, and of the various ways in which hearers are affected by it. To some its warbling is like the sound of a beautiful mysterious instrument, while to others it seems like the singing of a blithe-hearted child with a highly melodious voice. I had often heard and listened with delight to the singing of the rialejo in the Guayana forests, but this song, or musical phrase, was utterly unlike it in character. It was purer, more expressive, softer—so low that at a distance of forty yards I could hardly have heard it. But its greatest charm was its resemblance to the human voice—a voice purified and brightened to something almost angelic.

But the materialization of Rima is diasppointing, partly, no doubt, because we have expected so much. She is neither spirit, nor bird, nor complete human being; and it is difficult to love her or understand Abel's passions for her.

The worst examples of the undue prolongation of slender material is the long section dealing with the journey to Riolama. It not only holds up the movement of the story but seems entirely unnecessary. Doubtless it was introduced as an excuse for the unsatisfactory love scene with which it culminates—a scene in which not only the evocation of the erotic emotion but the language the lovers address to each other has a peculiarly false ring.

> My love, my life, my sweet Rima, I know that you will understand me now as you did not before, on that dark night—you do remember it, Rima?—when I held you clasped to my breast in the wood. How it pierced my heart with pain to speak plainly to you as I did on the mountain to-night—to kill the hope that had sustained and brought you so far from home! But now that anguish is over; the shadow had gone out of those beautiful eyes that are looking at me.

This is second-hand stuff. There is a melodramatic touch about it almost reminiscent of a Victorian 'heavy.' The whole of the middle part of the book is marred by this kind of writing—in contrast to the fine beginning and end.

One of the most odd passages in the book is that in which Hudson describes the finding by Abel of Rima's remains under the tree in which the Indians had burned her.

> At noon on the following day I found the skeleton, or, at all events, the larger bones, rendered so fragile by the fierce heat they had been subjected to, that they fell to pieces when handled. But I was careful—how careful!—to save these last sacred relics, all that was now left of Rima!—kissing each white fragment as I lifted it, and gathering them all in my old frayed cloak, spread out to receive them.

When we read this awkward yet strangely pathetic passage in its context we see that it is partly justified in relation to the circumstances. Abel is stunned and broken-hearted, and dark undertones of despair are suggested beneath his factual description of the finding of the bones. Hudson was faced with a problem in dealing with this important incident, a problem that he did not solve with entire success. The news of Rima's death and the discovery of the bones is, I take it, intended to be the supreme moment of the book. But we have already reached one peak—the passionate scenes at Riolama, and have before us another and greater—the despair and madness of Abel. Hudson was confronted by the almost insoluble problem of fitting his supreme moment between two climactic peaks. He attempted to solve it by toning down the death of Rima to the quietest shade. It is not seen by Abel, and therefore not directly experienced by the reader: it is described by the Indian after the event. As we have seen, the actual finding of the bones is reduced almost to a piece of reporting. But though in this section of the book he achieves his effect of restraint as a whole, he does it only at the expense of individual passages—as in the example quoted above with its crude and unnecessary 'at all events,' and its awkward 'rendered so fragile by the fierce heat they had been subjected to.' How an artist such as Hudson could have passed 'had been subjected to' at such a poignant moment is hard to understand. Nor does there seem any reason for the exclamation marks which not only increase the awkwardness of the passage, but destroy its poignancy with a wholly inexplicable suggestion of humour. Hudson wished to avoid over-statement and it led him to crude statement.

The final section of the book is, in my view, the best—as though with the removal of the artificial erotic element Hudson was at last able to give full rein to his imagination. In its fierce note of fantasy and tragedy it is akin to *Marta Riquelme*, and is surpassed nowhere else. Abel's desolation of spirit and his loneliness are heightened by the background of the sinister forest—sinister, now, after Rima's terrible death. His brooding insanity is depicted with remarkable power, and the chapter describing him alone in the crude hut he has built over the remains of Rima's old home with only a huge hairy spider for company, and feeling, in his madness, Rima's arms about him, is overwhelming in its grief and horror. The return journey of Abel, like so many incidents in the book, is rather prolonged, but it does not affect us in the same way as the prolongation of the earlier erotic passages. As a whole, *Green Mansions* leaves an indelible impression, and as a whole it is best judged. Its faults are many; but they are swallowed up in its originality and power.

Green Mansions was the last major work of fiction Hudson wrote. In the following year appeared a tale for children, *A Little Boy Lost*, and except for occasional short pieces, such as *Dead Man's Plack* (an historical tale of Edward the Martyr), the Downland tragedy, *An Old Thorn*, and some unpublished efforts, Hudson was henceforth to give all his energies to the perfecting of the essay form which was uniquely his own, and in which he expressed himself, not as a story-teller, but as a field naturalist.

In spite of great originality and, at times, high inspiration, Hudson's fiction is not altogether satisfying. Much of it represents a side of him that was alien from his integral self, and as such it is inferior to the Essays. Readers who first came to him through the Romances might not find it so; but to get to know him, as I did, through the Essays, is to feel the contrast acutely. The Essays do not make so great an immediate impact as the Romances, largely because they are less startling and seem less original; but to be original in describing nature and wild life is far harder than in inventing fantastic stories about a strange people in a distant land. In a subtle way the Essays are more original than the Romances, and in most cases they are more mature. The Romances are a great achievement; but they are not Hudson's greatest achievement or his most representative work.

THE ESSAYS

Every mode of creative expression is circumscribed by its own laws of structure and form; but all are not equally circumscribed. Music and architecture are perhaps the most dependent upon form. A symphony will be unsatisfactory if conceived in the form of a fantasia, and a railway station will be a bad piece of architecture if it resembles a Gothic cathedral. In sculpture there is more freedom; in painting still more; in literature—apart from verse—most of all. The freedom of literature allows for a considerable overlapping and interpenetration of its forms. Thus, so long as it contains a story of some kind, a novel may be a farrago, a piece of reporting, a psycho-biography, or an ideological *pastiche*, and yet be a satisfying work of literary art: a biography, providing it keeps to its human centre may take almost as many forms: literary criticism may be philosophical or aesthetic; and so on. But of the many interpenetrating forms of literature, the essay is the most free. Within the scope of an essay it is possible to include aspects of every other literary form as well as the author's entire philosophy and experience. His essay may be on any subject: it may include aspects of fiction, verse, scientific or philosophic speculation, and general information without being any the less a recognizable essay. Paradoxically, an essay may be defined as a literary form, the function of which is to be as informal as possible.

For a field naturalist such as Hudson who, as he said, took all life for his field, the essay was the ideal mode of expression. It was the perfect medium for his rich and observant mind. In the Romances he was constrained by plot and development: in the Essays he was free to be himself. The Essays are, on the whole, his most mature and characteristic work, containing the clearest expression of his outlook, his finest conceptions, and most sustained inspiration. At their best they are spacious, balanced, and serene, rich in imagination and fertile in ideas. Though relatively subdued as compared with the Romances, their emotional range is wide; and the moments of intensity are far more effective by contrast with their serene background of observation and description. The worst that can be said against the Essays is that they are dull in places. Hudson is occasionally content to record rather trite observations and stories in a level, somewhat colourless manner; and he was capable—very rarely—of being a bore.

The Essays follow no set pattern. They are free, discursive, and rambling. Each chapter or section is centred in a particular subject—a conversation with a countryman, a description of a village, or the song of a bird; but the subject is treated very freely, and used, in the true essay manner, as a jumping-off ground for ideas, reflections, and stories. The separate chapters or sections are in most cases linked together to form an organic whole. Hudson rarely planned an essay and sat down to write it. Out of the immense storehouse of his material he selected what he wanted and wove it around a central theme—a place, such as West Sussex in *Nature in Downland*; a person, as in *A Shepherd's Life*; or an idea, as in *A Hind in Richmond Park*. Many of his essays contain revised articles already published in newspapers and periodicals. But they were always related to his central theme—indeed the unity of his mind would have imparted a certain consistency to anything he had chosen to arrange. Objectively, nature holds together all his essays and gives unity to the material within each essay: subjectively, Hudson's own personality is the unifying element.

With three exceptions which deal with South America, the Essays are set in England, and reveal the essential Englishness of Hudson. In spite of his American-born father and American mother, and his birth and upbringing in South America, he was, as we have seen, fundamentally English, and the majority of his essays are among the most characteristically English writings, both in spirit and style, of our time.

The Essays reveal his power of transforming the simplest experiences and making us relive them with him; and when his inspiration is at the tide, the most commonplace events take on significance. This showed his originality far more vividly than did his capacity as a story-teller; for, as Disraeli said: 'The originality of a subject is in its treatment.' In the words of Charles Morgan: 'Treatment is the artist's means of drawing in his material, of converting it, and of giving it out again in a new form, instinct with himself, so that even the most deliberately objective art is distinguished from reporting by its being, not a representation of fact, but the artist's own truth, unique as he is unique.' Hudson's art in the Essays was primarily objective: he was the observing naturalist reporting what he saw. But once his material had passed through the crucible of his imagination it became transformed, 'instinct with himself,' and events that might otherwise have been trivial took on the significance of 'his own truth.' A superficial reader of Hudson's Essays might regard him merely as a sensitive reporter; but those who read with understanding and sympathy will mirror the brightness with which he illumined every common event in the light of his vision. The Essays are the true and integral expression of his art, and in them we shall find the essential Hudson.

Apart from the Essays, Hudson produced a few text-books, the chief surviving example of which is *British Birds* written in 1895. It was not altogether a success, and he did not attempt this sort of book again. His gifts as a naturalist were largely aesthetic, and were best expressed in the free essay form. The straightforward classification and description required by the text-book seemed to constrain him, just as did the demands of plot and development in the Romances. Furthermore he was not, as I have said, a scientific ornithologist, and *British Birds* cannot be described as entirely accurate or adequately comprehensive. As Roberts said: 'He will very seldom look at any text-book or compendium which gives general clues to all that has been written . . .' Such value as the book possesses lies in its vivid little portraits and impressions of the particular species Hudson himself knew. Even so, the treatment is far better in the Essays. I would also mention here the *Rare, Vanishing, and Lost British Birds* compiled by Linda Gardiner, a slight, but interesting curiosity. The early *Argentine Ornithology* (the scientific part of which was contributed by Professor Sclater) was revised and made less technical many years afterwards as *Birds of La Plata*.

Of Hudson's Essays, the two earliest, *The Naturalist in La Plata*, and *Idle Days in Patagonia*, were set in South America. *The Naturalist in La Plata* is concerned mainly with animal life, and Roberts tells us that it embodied many of the talks he had with Hudson in the garden of the Leinster Square boarding house during the early days of their friendship; and he adds that he could never read it without hearing 'the faint sounds of his speech.' *Idle Days* contains 'The War with Nature' chapter (part of which I quoted earlier) which was a development of an essay, 'The Settler's Recompense,' originally published in a defunct magazine called *Merry England*. It was the first book to deal fully with the question of animism—a subject that so often recurred in later works. In spite of their aesthetic character, both books seem to have made some impression in the scientific world. Then came *Birds in a Village*, the first of the English essays, long afterwards revised and developed as *Birds in Town and Village*. I shall consider it later in this form.

Though charming in places, the next book, *Birds in*

London, lacks interest to-day, chiefly on account of the fact that owing to the changing face of London so much of it has become out of date. Whatever may have been Hudson's conscious attitude to London—and we have seen that it was very enigmatical—he was evidently not inspired by it if we may judge from this book. The atmosphere of bricks and mortar, parks, and waste land is enervating, and much of the book is dull and second-rate.

Its successor, *Nature in Downland*, was Hudson's first mature and genuinely characteristic English essay, and became the pattern of all his subsequent writings in this sphere. In it he found his true mode of expression; and with the exception of *Birds of La Plata* all his remaining essays are set in the English countryside.

When Hudson wrote *Nature in Downland* he had already published eight full-length works—three novels, four essays, and a text-book—and had reached full maturity. It is essentially English, and reveals all his wonderful power of capturing and expressing the spirit of our landscape. The rambling but coherent structure is very characteristic. Its setting is for many of us one of the most typical corners of England, one that, in spite of exploitation by business men, artists, writers, stage folk, and week-enders generally, still retains its charm and freshness. Hudson's downland is West Sussex, which, as the poet says, 'is best Sussex.' He must have steeped himself in it, for the writing is so vivid at times that it seems to take us beyond the imagination into the realm of actual sensation. He makes us almost physically experience the downland landscape in summer—the colours and scent of flowers, the songs of birds, the cries of sheep and the far-off tolling of bells, blue sky and silver sea, and thistledown floating in the hot, shimmering air.

The bees buzzing in the downland air are not more insistent than those buzzing in Hudson's bonnet. Chief of them is the Chichester drink trade. All Hudson could see in Chichester was its innumerable inns and public-houses

—a strange myopia in a man of such artistic sensibility, for it is a gem of a town in a lovely setting. Eric Gill, who as a boy lived in Chichester, gives a very different picture in his *Autobiography*: he appreciated its beautiful medieval proportions and was deeply alive to its continuity and sense of tradition. But Hudson saw only drink and poverty. He remarks with scorn that in a town of 12,000 souls and an adult population of 3,000 'there are seventy public-houses, besides several wine and spirit merchants, and grocers with licences.' All this may be very interesting to the statistician and social reformer, but it is rather out of place in an open-air book. It is not, however, inconsistent with Hudson's attitude to life. His bright and acute senses and fecundity of imagination needed no stimulant, and though he was himself a moderate drinker he shrank in horror from the lowering and degrading effect of alcohol which, taken to excess, coarsens sensibility and weakens the powers of the imagination. For Hudson, drink was the real 'opium of the people,' chaining them down in darkness and making impossible that development of the imagination which, he believed, was essential to happiness—though why he should have selected Chichester in particular, and why he should have been so blind to the charm of the place, is something of a mystery.

Perhaps his aversion to the town had a more personal and emotional origin, and may be traceable to the effect of an incident he records in *Nature in Downland*. At an inn where he was staying they kept three captive birds, jackdaw, blackbird, and owl, the first two confined in small hutch-like cages in a dimly-lit passage. The owl was cooped up in a dirty uncovered cage in the kitchen where a fire was burning continually, and in addition to this discomfort, he was tortured by the fierce stabbing light of the gas jets around him. Hudson tried hard to get the landlady to release him, and at last she promised to do so. But for some reason or other she changed her mind—and 'from that time,' says Hudson, 'I was afraid to go near him. . . .' The bird 's reproachful image like 'a feathered Dreyfus, Semitic features and all, the head bowed, the weary eyes closed, the hooked nose just visible amidst a wilderness of white whiskers' haunted him. It is easy to understand the feelings such things aroused in one who so delighted in the incomparable beauty and freedom of bird life. One of his most moving short essays, 'A Linnet for Sixpence' (published in Edward Garnett's *Hudson Anthology*), deals with this subject of captive birds, and tells of a linnet, destined for captivity, which he bought from a street seller in London. He took it home, intending to release it; but it died almost immediately. Packing it in a box he carried it out into the open country where it had once loved and sung, and buried it under a furze bush. In those days it was fashionable for women to wear exotic birds in their hats. The sight filled Hudson with anger, though unlike so many who are moved in this way he was never fanatical. He never lost his sense of proportion; and when an over-zealous lady, fired by his writing on the Chichester owl, begged him to use his influence to release an owl chained up in the garden of a country house, he refused to interfere.

The Chichester incidents take up a comparatively small part of *Nature in Downland*, which is essentially a nature book. If Hudson had written no other essay it would have been outstanding; but it is rather overshadowed by some of the later works.

It was followed by *Birds and Man*—a book that Hudson revised and reissued long afterwards, in 1915. Though not one of his greatest essays it contains some individual chapters of very high quality, particularly those dealing with the charm of bird song and wild flowers. Hudson explains this charm as due to human association. He instances the human-like timbre of the willow wren's song, quoting Warde Fowler on the rhythmic resemblance of bird song to human conversation rather than to music. This resemblance, as I pointed out earlier in discussing family relationship, is very evident in the warbler family. But Hudson differs from Fowler in believing that the human association is less a question of rhythm than of a human-like quality of sound, as in the blackbird, swallow, pied wagtail, blackcap, linnet, and tree pipit. The discussion is enchanting, and leads to speculations on human association in the charm of flowers. This Hudson puts down to expression and colour—by expression meaning some aspect of a flower that calls forth such names as 'love-in-a-mist,' 'forget-me-not,' and so on. 'Not books,' he writes, 'but the light of nature, the experience of our own early years, the look which no person not blinded by reading can fail to see in a flower, ia sufficient to reveal all this hidden wonderful knowledge about the first openings of the heart towards nature, during the remote infancy of the human race.' He goes on to consider the association of colour and charm—a passage that has to be read in all its aesthetic and intellectual richness to be fully appreciated.

In *Birds and Man* Hudson has a good deal to say about the furze wren, or Dartford warbler. He had a great affection for this beautiful little bird, with its minute, sturdy body, crested head, and long tail, and returned to it in several of his books. It was never a common species, and was rare during Hudson's lifetime. But in the twenties it increased in numbers, and for some years I could always be sure of finding it—a restless 'slate-black and chestnut-red' figure, flitting among the furze bushes and occasionally singing its 'queer little fizgig of a song'—on certain lonely stretches of heath in the south of England. Now, at the time of writing, it has become rare again. When Hudson wrote, its rarity was largely due to the depredations of the collector; but its present rarity is said to have been caused by the excessively cold winters of 1938 to 1940, which cut off its food supply.

This question of food supply raises an interesting problem relative to migration. The Dartford warbler is our one resident warbler. Its cousin, the great whitethroat, who resembles it in the 'square' bodily form (though with different coloration and without the crest and long tail) has a not dissimilar environment and food. Yet the whitethroat migrates, while the more delicate furze wren remains to face the rigours of a northern winter. Now I think the question is not why does the whitethroat migrate? but why does the Dartford warbler *not* migrate? Migration, in some form or another, seems natural to all living creatures, and can be regarded as a manifestation of universal energy or as an impulse reflecting the evolutionary movement of life. In man, where the mind is most developed, migration mainly takes the form of voyaging in the realm of the imagination or exploring the world of ideas, though physical migration still plays a part. The extraordinary persistence of aggressive wars in Germany may partly be explained as due to a migratory urge. At all events, there seems good reason to think that non-migration, physically and mentally, is exceptional. If so, it may be that the rarity of the Dartford warbler is due to something less obvious than the man with a gun, or a lack of food. It may be due to a recessive tendency that is at the same time responsible for its non-migration, though why and how this recessive tendency should come about I am unable to suggest. The only way to tackle the problem would be to discover whether species tend to die out as they become less migratory.

Hudson's devotion to the elusive little furze wren led him to protest against the aesthetic absurdity of a bird so animated and ethereal in a glass case. In the first chapter of *Birds and Man* he writes contemptuously of the anomaly of stuffed birds, arguing that the essential character of such warm-blooded creatures is their animation. Although museum specimens are necessary for study, aesthetically they are a mockery—a collection of 'ancient, dusty, dead little birds, painful to look at—a libel on nature and an insult to man's intelligence.' Later on, he returns to the subject and gives us the most inspired and original chapter in the book, and one of the strangest and most fantastic things in the entire range of his work—an imaginary dialogue between a stuffed squirrel and woodpecker in the sitting-room of a lonely cottage in Cornwall. The title of the chapter, 'Something Pretty in a Glass Case,' gives no indication of what is to come, and at first its irony is not apparent.

On that 'furthermost, lonely, melancholy coast' of the Land's End a tremendous gale was blowing. Several times during the day he had tried to go out and face it, but he was always driven back. 'From time to time I get up and look through the window-pane at the few cold, grey naked cottages and empty bleak fields, divided by naked grey stone fences, and, beyond the fields, the foam-flecked, colder, greyer, more desolate ocean.' He imagines the bushes growing in the west country in April—and while solacing himself with these memories, his attention is suddenly riveted upon two glass cases, one containing a squirrel and the other a green woodpecker. Sitting there in the failing light with the gale howling outside, he watches them, and presently begins to imagine that he can hear them addressing each other. There follows a mountingly terrifying dialogue between the two lifeless and mummified objects, who hate each other. Finally, when their invective is spent, they turn their hate upon him, and with ghastly malignancy suggest that he is going mad. 'Suddenly their sharp agitated voices fell to a broken whispering and died into silence. For the wind had lulled again. Looking closely at them I thought I could see a new expression in their immovable glass eyes. It frightened me, I began to be frightened at myself; for it seemed to me now that I really was becoming insane, and I was suddenly seized with a fierce desire to snatch the cases down and crush them into the fire with my heel. To save myself from such a mad act I jumped up, and picking up my candle, hurried upstairs to my bedroom'—there to be visited with terrible dreams of the squirrel and the woodpecker, and of men, stuffed, and set up in niches in the walls of the palace of hell.

The fantastic 'otherness' of this Dialogue of the Dead, as Hudson calls it, is greatly increased by the background of nature in her wildest mood—the fury of the wind and the sea, the menacing darkness, the desolate coast. In such a passage—which recalls some of the more horrific writing in the Romances, but is more convincing, more genuine, more integrally Hudson—we can see the manifestation of his Celtic inheritance.

His next book of essays, *Hampshire Days*, is one of the most satisfying from every angle. At the start we are arrested by a brilliant chapter on the young cuckoo—a marvellous example of his power of sustained observation and attention. One afternoon in May a cuckoo hatched out of a robin's nest containing three robin's eggs, and all during the following afternoon and throughout the whole of the next day Hudson kept watch upon the nest. He observed that the newly hatched cuckoo ejected the robins' eggs automatically in response to irritation, which began against its sides, increased near the upper surface, and was most intense in the hollow of the back. The constant fidgeting gradually rolled the egg into the hollow, where the irritation became intolerable, and at last, with an immense effort, the young cuckoo raised its back and jerked the egg out of the nest. The same process was applied to the newly hatched foster brothers. Hudson concluded that the irritability is an inherited condition for getting rid of the cuckoo's rivals. It begins to disappear soon after they are all ejected—as he proved to his own satisfaction by trying the cuckoo with an egg or pebble in his back for several days after the last ejection.

The cuckoo incident is only one of the many admirable things in *Hampshire Days*, a book of immense variety, ranging over a wide field of experience. It contains what is perhaps the greatest passage in all Hudson, describing the emotions and thoughts aroused by an ancient burial place of the prehistoric dead. The passage derives its power from the intensity of Hudson's atavistic identification of himself with the men of that distant time. For the moment he is at one with them—the long-forgotten race who left their barrows and monoliths as an everlasting memorial.

Here, sheltered by the bushes, I sat and saw the sun go down, and the long twilight deepen till the oak woods of Beaulieu in the west looked black on the horizon, and the stars came out: in spite of the cold wind that made me shiver in my thin clothes, I sat there for hours, held by the silence and solitariness of that mound of the ancient dead.

Sitting there, profoundly sad for no apparent cause, with no conscious thought in my mind, it suddenly occurred to me that I had known that spot from of old, that in long-past forgotten years I had often come there of an evening and sat through the twilight, in love with the loneliness and peace, wishing that it might be my last resting-place. To sleep there for ever—the sleep that knows no waking! We say it, but do not mean—do not believe it. Dreams do come to give us pause; and we know that we have lived. To dwell alone, then, with this memory of life in such a spot for all time! There are moments in which the thought of death steals upon and takes us as it were by surprise, and it is then exceeding bitter. It was as if that cold wind blowing over and making strange whispers in the heather had brought a sudden tempest of icy rain to wet and chill me.

This miserable sensation soon passed away, and, with quieted heart, I began to grow more and more attracted by the thought of resting on so blessed a spot. To have always about me that wildness which I best loved—the rude incult heath, the beautiful desolation; to have harsh furze and ling and bramble and bracken to grow on me, and only wild creatures for visitors and company. The little stonechat, the tinkling meadow-pipit, the excited whitethroat to sing to me in summer; the deep-burrowing rabbit to bring down his warmth and familiar smell among my bones; the heat-loving adder, rich in colour, to find when summer is gone a dry safe shelter and hibernaculum in my empty skull.

So beautiful did the thought appear that I could have laid down my life at that moment, in spite of death's bitterness, if by so doing I could have had my desire. But no such sweet and desirable a thing could be given me by this people and race that pos sess the earth, who are not like the people here with me in the twilight on the heath. For I thought, too, of those I should lie with, having with them my after life; and thinking of them I was no longer alone. I thought of them not as others think, those others of a strange race. What *do* they think? They think so many things! The materialist, the scientist, would say: They have no existence; they ceased to be anything when their flesh was turned to dust, or burned to ashes, and their minds, or souls, were changed to some other form of energy, or motion, or affection of matter, or whatever they call it. The believer would not say of them, or of the immaterial part of them, that they had gone into a world of light, that in a dream or vision he had seen them walking in an air of glory; but he might hold that they had been preached to in Hades some nineteen centuries ago, and had perhaps repented of their barbarous deeds. Or he might think, since he has considerable latitude allowed him on the point, that the imperishable parts of them are here at this very spot, tangled in dust that was once flesh and bones, sleeping like chrysalids through a long winter, to be raised again at the sound of a trumpet blown by an angel to a second conscious life, happy or miserable as may be willed.

I imagine none of these things, for they were with me in the twilight on the barrow in crowds, sitting and standing in groups, and many lying on their sides on the turf below, their heads resting in their hands. They, too, all had their faces turned towards Beaulieu. Evening by evening for many and many a century they had looked to that point, towards the black wood on the horizon, where there were people and sounds of human life. Day by day for centuries they had listened with wonder and fear to the Abbey bells, and to the distant chanting of the monks. And the Abbey has been in ruins for centuries, open to the sky and overgrown with ivy; but still towards that point they look with apprehension, since men still dwell there, strangers to them, the little busy eager people, hateful in their artificial indoor lives; who do not know and who care nothing for them, who worship not and fear not the dead that are underground, but dig up their sacred places and scatter their bones and ashes, and despise and mock them because they are dead and powerless.

It is not strange that they fear and hate. I look at them—their dark, pale, furious faces—and think that if they could be visible thus in the daylight, all who came to that spot or passed near it would turn and fly with a terrifying image in their mind which would last to the end of life. But they do not resent my presence, and would not resent it were I permitted to come at last to dwell with them for ever.

I have quoted at some length because this passage contains, more than any other that I know, the quintessential Hudson. He never wrote anything more characteristic and personal. Even his failings and peculiarities are here, transcended in the marvellous inspiration of the whole. Only when we read the passage very carefully with deliberate critical intent do we become aware of certain obscurities such as occur in the second to the fifth sentences of paragraph two about dreams and death, and certain crudities, as in the fourth to the seventh sentences of paragraph four with its confusion of 'they,' the moderns, and 'they,' the ancient men, and the unnecessary repetition of the word 'or' in sentences seven and eight. But we do not ordinarily notice these things: we share Hudson's experience, and are carried along with him. The way in which the passage is built up, beginning quietly on a tender, sorrowful note, and gradually increasing in intensity to the end, is masterly. All Hudson is here: his feeling of unity with the earth—the bliss of lying for ever in that rude, wild place, with the stonechat and rabbit for company, and the adder curled up in his empty skull: his contempt for materialism; his religious doubt—the old problem of immortality that had vexed him since childhood: and the atavistic primitivism that inspired the whole tremendous passage.

Elsewhere in *Hampshire Days* he deals at some length with racial types—a subject that interested him continually.

He speaks of the persistence of the dark Iberian type in certain areas, and of T. H. Huxley's contention that 'the English people generally are not Saxons in the shape of the head.' According to Hudson, the divergence of types is greatest in Hampshire. In the southern half of the county the dark people are almost as common as the blond.

Hudson's observations led him to regard the English as a very mixed race; and in view of the evidence it seems remarkable that the myth of the Saxon Englishman should have taken such a hold and survived for so long. It probably originated in the religious prejudice in favour of German Protestantism, but was greatly strengthened by the German influence at court, beginning with the first George and culminating in the unofficial reign of the Prince Consort. From the court it spread to the governing classes, and from thence to the universities where it was developed and rationalized, and from the universities it reached the press and the schools and finally the people. By the close of the Victorian era it was firmly believed that we, the English and German peoples, were all 'one glorious and conquering teutonic race.' Yet there seems little evidence for it from either anthropology, history, or experience. Anthropologically, Huxley's remarks on the skull have been amply confirmed. Historically, it is no longer possible to believe that the sturdy Saxons overran Britain in vast hordes, exterminating most of the small population, and driving the remainder into Wales where they have been bottled up ever since. The native population is now believed to be larger than was formerly estimated, and, in any case, the evidence for the numbers of the invaders is very fragmentary. Certainly they were not the 'vast hordes' of Victorian history. The invaders influenced us considerably: they completely overran some parts of the country (mostly near the coast) and they married freely with the natives. But they merged into great parts of the population and were absorbed into its life as a whole.

Empirically, the evidence is entirely contrary to the Saxon myth. Thus the German attitude to authority is servile and worshipping while our own is independent (although, having a strong social sense, we are able to live peacefully under a loose aristocratic democracy): the Germans are a humourless people while we are notorious for our humour: the Germans are painstakingly thorough, but we are muddlers: Germany produces great metaphysical philosophers and musicians, but we produce little philosophy (and that mainly empirical) and until recently were known as the most unmusical nation in Europe. But although there is little resemblance between Germans and Englishmen there *is* an underlying racial unity between the peoples of the British islands, the basis of which appears to be Celtic, as Hudson's observations bear out. If this is so, English independence may be regarded as a tempered form of Celtic rebelliousness, English humour of Celtic horse-play, and English imagination of Celtic fantasy; although, since mixing produces a new element, we are, in the long run, neither Celt, Saxon, Dane, or Norman, but English—a peculiar people on our own.

Hudson returned to the question of racial types in his next book of essays, *The Land's End.* He seems to have had a preference for the dark, Celtic type. It 'may be due to the Celtic element in me,' he writes, 'that I feel very much at home with the [Cornish] people. A Dumnonian, if not a "swart Belerian," with an admixture of Irish blood, I feel myself related to them. . . .' But though he liked the Cornish, he does not seem greatly to have admired them. He thought they lacked humour. 'But I am not saying there is no humour in Cornwall. There may be such a thing; but if you meet with it you will find that it is of the ordinary sort, only of an inferior quality, and that there is very little.' He was much put off by the harshness of their particular brand of religion with its ugly churches, revivalist hysteria, and 'the prayers of the man who, with "odious familiarity" buttonholes the Deity,' and he remarks that 'one may be thankful that the Irish kept the old faith, which does not permit such things. . . .' Indifference to beauty saddened and angered him: he could not fathom the mentality that associates the worship of God with a bare-walled tin chapel. *The Land's End*, though perhaps not one of his greatest essays, gives many vivid pictures of Cornwall, its people, landscape, and natural history. It is very typical; but there is not much that can be said of it in detail.

The same applies to the essay which followed, *Afoot in England*—a serene and mature book. The writing is on a high level; but it is not very inspired and has few outstanding passages. Most of it is set in the west country, and there are charming impressions of Salisbury, Wells, and Bath. On the whole, the human and scenic interest predominates. It was followed, a year later, by *A Shepherd's Life*, his most famous essay, and one of the most distinguished of all his works.

A Shepherd's Life is Hudson's best known essay, and probably his best known book after *Green Mansions*. It is already regarded as a classic; and I can think of no other book of his that approaches it in sustained beauty and serenity. Although almost everything he wrote contains something of value, his work, like that of most great men, was uneven; but *A Shepherd's Life* stands apart in being of even quality throughout. It is not, perhaps, his greatest, but it is certainly his most perfect book—a flawless thing, unique, complete, and final. Its quietude never becomes dull, and though it lacks the emotional intensity and intellectual fecundity of some of the other works, it is pervaded by a glowing coolness that imparts to it the quality of an autumnal sunset.

Edward Garnett quotes a letter from Hudson on *A Shepherd's Life*.

You said so much in praise of *A Shepherd's Life* I had to wait and get cool before replying. But you are always too generous to me. The reason of it is that you are to some extent under an illusion. A man is so much better than his books!—Take the best thing you have done—don't you feel how little of all the best in you it contains—and that little how poorly expressed? I don't like even to look at a book of mine after it is finished. I suppose when you know a man intimately and have an affection for him, you get into the way of expecting to find him—something worthy of him—in his book. Hence the illusion.

And Garnett adds: 'How like Hudson to deprecate *A Shepherd's Life*!—that rich intimate web, so strongly woven, that truthful tapestry of the ways, facts, manners, and character of the life of the old-world people of the Wiltshire Downs.' But Hudson was not so much deprecating *A Shepherd's Life* as lamenting the inadequacy of any art-form to express the full experience of the artist. No artist can see his finished work in perspective. Many overrate what they have written; some underrate it; a few are indifferent. But I think that, like Hudson, most artists enjoy mainly the act of creation and are dissatisfied with what they have written when it is done. 'No sooner have I finished a book, than I come, rover-like, to hate it,' he says in the last sentence of the last book he ever wrote.

The setting of *A Shepherd's Life* is a Wiltshire village called by Hudson 'Winterbourne Bishop.' He never disclosed the real name of the village, but gave Roberts a clue when he told him there was a Bustard House and a Bustard Down near by. Recently, however, there appeared in the correspondence columns of *The Times Literary Supplement* an interesting letter purporting to give, not only the name of the village, but also of the shepherd around whom the book is written—Caleb Bawcombe, as Hudson called him. The village, says the writer, is Martin, on the borders of Hampshire, Wiltshire, and Dorset; and extracts from the church register make it possible to identify Caleb Bawcombe. 'Isaac Bawcombe, father of Caleb, was . . .

an only child . . . born in 1800, and he and his wife died within a year of each other in 1886 . . . Their son, Caleb, was lame for life and his wife . . . temporarily left him to start a little business of her own . . .' There is also 'a description of a lawsuit brought against Elijah Raven for the recovery of sick pay from the Village Benefit Club in which Caleb Bawcombe was the principle witness.' The writer discovered that there was a 'William Lawes, shepherd, . . . an only son, born 1800. In 1823 he married Mary Upjohn, by whom he had four children, the eldest, James, born in 1827. William Lawes died in March 1886, his wife in December of the same year. James Lawes is still remembered as having walked with a limp and his wife as having set up a business on her own.' Finally, in the writer's view, the 'identification of Caleb Bawcombe with James Lawes is established with certainty by the discovery among the papers in the vestry of an account from a firm of solicitors in Salisbury for six-and-eightpence for taking an affidavit from James Lawes in the case against Malachi Martin, who corresponds in every particular with Elijah Raven of the book.'

Winterbourne Bishop, or Martin, seems to be an unexceptional place by any standard. Hudson tells us that although 'of the few widely separated villages, hidden away among the lonely downs' he loved Winterbourne Bishop the best, yet 'it would be pronounced by most persons the least attractive.' It had little shade from trees in summer and was exposed to the wind in winter. A long winding street ran through it, 'with a green bank, five or six feet high, on either side, on which stand the cottages,' for the most part commonplace and undistinguished. In summer the village is waterless, and the bed of the stream lying beside the bank is full of rubbish and dust and overgrown with dock and nettles. 'No,' Hudson adds, 'I cannot think that any person for whom it had no association, no secret interest, would, after looking at this village with its dried-up winterbourne, care to make his home in it.' But he possessed that secret, which lay in the hearts of those who for generations had lived in the village and created its personality. In communicating the secret to us he makes us share his love for the place, and to see it, as he saw it, glowing with the light of imaginative memory.

Much of the book is made up of stories told by Caleb Bawcombe relating to the history and occupations of his family and neighbours in the village and surrounding countryside. The incidents recorded are simple enough, and concern mainly the everyday work, loves, sorrows, and joys of the country people; but they are transformed and transmuted within the crucible of Hudson's imagination. He does not invent anything: he takes what is already there and, in the mere act of taking, transforms it. More than any other book of his, *A Shepherd's Life* bears out the truth we considered earlier on in connection with Morgan's words on treatment. Superficially, it could be described as a faithful record of Wiltshire life, written with sympathy and charm. Such a description would be correct—and totally inadequate. It would tell us nothing of the art that turned each trivial narrative into a thing of beauty, and made of the whole a flawless unity.

The human note is predominant in *A Shepherd's Life*, which contains many fine examples of character drawing, some of the most memorable done with a few strokes of the pen. Hudson never strains after effect in describing human personality. Sometimes he does not describe directly at all and the personality emerges obliquely from a number of impersonal incidents. All the characters of this book live unforgettably for us—Caleb and his brothers and sisters, his father Isaac, Liddy, old Elijah Raven the 'dictator' of the village, and, for me especially, Tommy Ierat who shepherded up to the age of seventy-eight. Early one Sunday afternoon when his wife was ill with influenza, old Tom came home, and 'putting aside his crook said: "I 've done work."'

'It 's early,' she replied, 'but maybe you got the boy to mind the sheep for you.'

'I don't mean I 've done work for the day,' he returned. 'I 've done for good—I 'll not go with the flock no more.'

'What be saying?' she cried in sudden alarm. 'Be you feeling bad—what be the matter?'

'No, I 'm not bad,' he said. 'I 'm perfectly well, but I 've done work;' and more than that he would not say.

She watched him anxiously but could see nothing wrong with him; his appetite was good, he smoked his pipe, and was cheerful.

Three days later she noticed that he had some difficulty in pulling on a stocking when dressing in the morning, and went to his assistance.

He laughed and said, 'Here 's a funny thing! You be ill and I be well, and you 've got to help me put on a stocking!' and he laughed again.

After dinner that day he said he wanted a drink and would have a glass of beer. There was no beer in the house, and she asked him if he would have a cup of tea.

'Oh, yes, that 'll do very well,' he said, and she made it for him.

After drinking his cup of tea he got a footstool, and placing it at her feet sat down on it and rested his head on her knees; he remained a long time in this position so perfectly still that she at length bent over and felt and examined his face, only to discover that he was dead.

And that was the end of Tommy Ierat, the son of Ellen. He died, she said, like a baby that has been fed and falls asleep on its mother's breast.

Hudson is far less discursive than usual in this book: most of the stories and incidents radiate from the village and the shepherd. There are stories of the old people of the village and of their youth long ago, many of them dealing with poaching and deer-stealing. In those days the agricultural labourer was underpaid and underfed, and though he was, in the main, honest and steady in his work, he did not regard the taking of animal flesh for the needs of his family as theft. He risked much, for the penalties were heavy. Reading some of the stories of poverty and oppression recorded in *A Shepherd's Life* we are filled with admiration for the endurance of the countryman of the early and middle nineteenth century. Yet in spite of his sufferings he succeeded in living a full and happy life—as Caleb Bawcombe's words bear so eloquent a testimony:

'I don't say that I want to have my life again, because 'twould be sinful. We must take what is sent. But if 'twas offered to me and I was told to choose my work, I 'd say, Give me my Wiltsheer Downs again and let me be a shepherd there all my life long.'

Caleb's philosophy is Hudson's also; that is why, in writing of a shepherd's life, he brings such inspired conviction to the task. He, too, wanted nothing but to live always close to nature and to enjoy the simple things; hence he was able to enter imaginatively into the shepherd's mind and feel at one with him in his hardships and sufferings.

The power of the countryman to rise above the most terrible hardship proceeds from his faith and courage—for it is not hardship that makes for unhappiness, but a drying up of the human spirit. The simple faith of the villagers gave them hope, and the constant presence of nature stabilized and strengthened them. Nothing else could have enabled them to live down such experiences as Hudson relates—the political struggles and riots in the early days of mechanization, and the cruel sentences of unfeeling judges who deported numberless men for life, never to see their loved ones again. In these pages Hudson comes nearer to the expression of a sociological attitude than anywhere else in his work. We have seen that he was, broadly speaking, a conservative; but his fundamental sociological attitude was more akin to what is called distributism; and the ideal that emerges from this book, older than any political system and to some extent entering into them all, is the ideal of well-distributed property and of small ownership, with its protest against monopoly in any form, capitalist or socialist. In the nineteenth century the countryman was everywhere attacked by machinery, the law, and the State, and much of *A Shepherd's Life* is a melancholy record of the encroachment of these forces and a protest against them. The protest is all the more effective because cast in aesthetic form; for where the abstract political treatise fails, a 'human story,' told with sympathy by a man of genius, will succeed.

Hudson's sympathy with the poor and illiterate countryman did not prevent him from appreciating the good points of the squire. He was able to feel at home with both shepherd and squire. The primitive and aristocratic appealed to the two sides of him which were revealed in his appearance, with its mixture of ruggedness and sensitive courtesy. His keen interest in human nature made it possible for him to get on with almost every type of man, no matter what his outlook or calling; but the most difficult for him to approach were the industrial proletarian and the business man. In the country labourer at one end, and the squire, artist, or man of letters at the other, he found elements of his own nature. H. J. Massingham has remarked on the affinity which unites the humblest agricultural worker with the squire. It is, he says, the land itself. Centuries of contact with the land have bred in each a love of a common thing that unites them beyond any distinctions of class or station. Hence rural societies seldom rebel, for between the squire and his men there is, in a literal sense, a natural bond, a bond of nature, whereas between the capitalist and the dispossessed proletarian there is only the antagonistic relation of impersonal economic forces.

Hudson was not blind to the dark side of the 'squirearchy.' Roberts observes that 'those who have read *A Shepherd's Life* will see how bitterly indignant he could be with the abuses that are too commonly connected with the ownership of land. He had seen tyranny in action. The type of Conservative landowner who was to him a noble and desirable animal to preserve was one who preserved the peasant and preferred healthy children to many head of game: one who did not encourage the breed of gamekeepers: who did not collect or destroy birds, who hated a pole-trap and an owl or a jay-murderer worse than a trespassing old woman seeking fallen firewood: one who was an ideal, kindly gentleman who thought more of humanity than of sport, who gloried in the varied life possible upon his estate and sought to increase it. It may be left to others to determine how many there are of the kind that appealed to him, as they and their fellows are displaced by rich men without the authority of ancestry or of manner or any true culture in their veins.' One would agree with Roberts in lamenting the displacement of the best type of aristocratic landowner by the rich; but it is not so much the rich man 'without the authority of ancestry' who has made things difficult for the countryman and, indeed, for the poor everywhere, but his successor, the bureaucrat, neither aristocratic nor wealthy, but powerful with all the power the State can confer.

A Shepherd's Life contains several intimate and charming portraits of squires, who, with all their faults and eccentricities, are, to my mind, the best of England. At the other end of the social scale are the sketches of gypsy life on the downs. The gypsy always fascinated Hudson. To many people he must have appeared something of a gypsy himself—a wanderer over the countryside, a rugged, weather-beaten figure, unique, beyond the artificial distinctions of class. He felt a genuine affinity with this ancient people, who, like himself, possessed an extraordinary sharpness and brightness of the senses. He was always happy and at ease in their company, and relates how he haunted their camp and had many talks with them. It is not difficult to understand their attraction which, for most of us, probably derives from the fact that they embody the hidden longing for lawless freedom and a life of primitive simplicity that exists deep in the human heart. We are no less attracted by the element of mystery revealed in their folk-lore and melancholy music, and in their strange prophetic powers to which Brian Vesey-Fitzgerald pays so remarkable a tribute in his book, *British Gypsies*. For centuries the gypsies of Britain have wandered up and down the length and breadth of these islands, watching men and civilizations come and go. But they remain; and in a sense they are the true natives of Britain, akin to those ancient men who built their lonely barrows and monoliths long ago on the high, windswept hills.

In his chapter on the gypsies, Hudson raises again the question of racial type and distribution which he discussed more fully in *Hampshire Days* and *The Land's End*. The chapter, called 'The Dark People of the Village,' contains some interesting speculations on the subject, and some charming stories of dark people told him by Caleb. Hudson distinguished three types of dark people of three distinct races in the Wiltshire downs—the brown-skinned gypsy type with high cheek-bones, the white-skinned, round-headed type, probably the descendants of the Wilsetae, and the very dark, oval-faced descendants of the ancient British race.

As a naturalist, Hudson tended to view people anthropologically; but as a man he approached each individual with sympathy and understanding as the manifestation of a unique self hood. For him, man, though he may exist in many spheres of being, religious, social, anthropological, psychological, is primarily an individual—a view in which he differed from so many of his contemporaries who tend to ignore individuality and to see man exclusively in one or other of these spheres. Where the sense of individuality is lost, freedom and responsibility vanish, and human life becomes cheap, as we see in the totalitarian countries. Nevertheless, man's individuality is ineradicable, since it is of the very essence of his nature. In the lowest forms of life individuality hardly exists; but as we ascend, there is increased differentiation, first in families, then in genera, then in species, until the advent of man, a creature in whom individuality is so highly developed that each person is, in a sense, a complete species in himself. The totalitarian movements of our time represent the attempts of the forces of reaction to arrest the terrifying thrust forward into greater individuality; man is frightened and bewildered by the development of his self-hood (a development greatly accelerated by the rapid increase of his knowledge and experience in the last three hundred years), and instead of seeking a deeper integration in God and nature takes blind refuge in the mass. Nevertheless, individuality must continue to develop, though totalitarianism may cause a great deal of misery, and last for a very long time. The environment depicted by Hudson in *A Shepherd's Life* is a fertile breeding-ground for human personality. Contact with nature and the rhythm of the seasons nourishes the individual soul. The men and women who emerge from this book are poor and ignorant and often down-trodden; but they are unmistakably individuals.

Though mainly concerned with man, *A Shepherd's Life* contains some of Hudson's most satisfying descriptions of natural scenery, notably the vale of the Wylye. Much of this little-known valley, about half a mile to a mile in width, with the river Wylye running through it, is wooded with great trees, elm, beech, and ash, and hidden away in the deep woods are many remote villages and hamlets of which Hudson tells some interesting stories. But the best thing in the chapter called 'The Vale of the Wylye' is his description of the valley as a whole and its effect on him:

. . . Wherein, then, does the 'Wylye bourne' differ from these others, and what is its special attraction? It was only when I set myself to think about it, to analyse the feeling in my own mind, that I discovered the secret—that is, in my own case, for of its effect on others I cannot say anything. What I discovered was that the various elements of interest, all of which may be found in other chalk-stream valleys, are here concentrated, or comprised in a limited space, and seen together produce a combined effect on the mind. It is the narrowness of the valley and the nearness of the high downs standing over it on either side, with, at some points, the memorials of antiquity carved on their smooth surfaces, the barrows and lynchetts or terraces, and the vast green earth-works crowning their summit. Up here on the turf, even with the lark singing his shrill music in the blue heavens, you are with the prehistoric dead, yourself for the time one of that innumerable, unsubstantial multitude, invisible in the sun, so that the sheep travelling as they graze, and the shepherd following them, pass through their ranks without suspecting their presence. And from that elevation you look down upon the life of to-day—the visible life, so brief in the individual, which, like the swift silver stream beneath, yet flows on continuously from age to age and for ever. And even as you look down you hear, at that distance, the bell of the little hidden church tower telling the hour of noon, and quickly following, a shout of freedom and joy from many shrill voices of children just released from school. Woke to life by those sounds, and drawn down by them, you may sit to rest or sun yourself on the stone table of a tomb overgrown on its sides with moss, the two-century-old inscription well-nigh obliterated, in the little grass-grown, flowery churchyard which serves as village green and playground in that small centre of life, where the living and the dead exist in a neighbourly way together. For it is not here as in towns, where the dead are away and out of mind and the past cut off. And if after basking too long in the sun in that tree-sheltered spot you go into the little church to cool yourself, you will probably find in a dim corner not far from the altar a stone effigy of one of an older time; a knight in armour, perhaps a crusader with legs crossed, lying on his back, dimly seen in the dim light, with perhaps a coloured sunbeam on his upturned face. For this little church where the villagers worship is very old; Norman on Saxon foundations; and before they were ever laid there may have been a temple to some ancient god at that spot, or a Roman villa perhaps. Far older than Saxon foundations are found in the vale, and mosaic floors, still beautiful after lying buried so long.

The above is a perfect example of the cumulative effect of Hudson's style. Taken by themselves many of his sentences are quite ordinary, or even, as we saw in the passage on 'The Barrow on the Heath,' crude and obscure; but woven together they produce a total effect of great beauty and power. We rarely catch our breath over a particular phrase in Hudson: we are borne along on the music of his prose, its movement slowly deepening our emotional and intellectual satisfaction. The entire chapter on the vale of the Wylye is rounded off and completed by the above quotation which occurs very near the end, permeating our senses with the glittering sunlight on the hill-top, the tolling bell and distant laughter of children, the warm stone of the tomb, and the coolness of the church with its beam of coloured sunlight. In F. M. Ford's phrase, Hudson makes us physically aware of his experience.

A Shepherd's Life is a book of deep satisfaction, a book full of kindliness and peace. Shepherds and sheep-dogs, and the lonely downs in sun and wind and rain; family life; hardship and sorrow, joy and thankfulness—these are the strands from which its 'rich tapestry' is woven. The charm of the book is indefinable, but may derive partly from its enshrinement of memory at one remove. It is permeated, not by the direct remembrance of Hudson's own experience, but by the memories of the shepherd, remembered again by Hudson and transformed in the light of his imagination. Memories of memories; and the passing of things that shall be no more.

Except in the Autobiography and the *Hind*, Hudson never again reached the level of *A Shepherd's Life*—although there is a perceptible increase of richness and maturity in all his subsequent works. The next essay, *Adventures among Birds*, from which I quoted in the first chapter, is altogether admirable; but I shall not say much more about it here. Some of the best of it is concerned with Wells-next-the-Sea, on the Norfolk coast, with its lonely mud-flats and sand-hills 'rough with grey marram grass,' and flocks of wild geese flying over the silver line of the sea. The grandeur and mystery of many birds in flight and the sound and smell of the sea remain, for me, the most vivid impressions in a book that is rich in every aspect of bird life. It is one of the supreme examples of Hudson's genius for getting into the bird mind.

After the matchless Autobiography (to be considered in the next chapter) appeared a revision, with additions, of *Birds in a Village*, renamed *Birds in Town and Village*. Although for the lover of birds it ranks high in its wealth of information and interest, from the literary and artistic point of view it is not the best Hudson. But like all his work it contains many inspired moments. The chapter entitled 'Chanticleer' reveals his extraordinary sensibility in capturing the majesty and mystery that lies behind the commonest of country sounds—the crowing of cocks. It is a sound that few people appreciate. We either take it for granted and ignore it, or else we connect it with the feelings of irritability and dislike aroused by its waking us in the early morning. But I doubt if any one with a grain of imagination would continue in this attitude after reading Hudson's chapter. He detects an astonishing range of colour in the voices of different cocks—a range absolutely unsuspected by the ordinary listener. All his wonderful power of association of ideas is here: he touches on science, history, poetry, and painting, and introduces a story, while all the time vividly analysing the call of chanticleer.

The Book of a Naturalist which followed is not one of the best known of Hudson's essays—inexplicably, for to my mind it is one of his most satisfying. It is wholly characteristic. There are few books of his for which I have more personal affection, perhaps because it was one of the first I ever read. I discovered it, many years ago, on the bookshelf of a cottage at which I was staying, and read it in ideal circumstances. Subsequent intimacy with Hudson's work as a whole has not changed my opinion of its high qualities. It deals mainly with mammals, reptiles, and insects. Birds are not to the fore—and even the noble heron is considered as a table bird. The incident of the heron is such a perfect example of Hudson's quiet, restrained but most effective humour that it will bear retelling.

The story concerns two timid, old-fashioned spinsters who related it to Hudson while he was on a visit to Bath. At one time they lived on a small farm on the Welsh coast with a bachelor brother who fancied himself as a sportsman, and was firmly convinced that most birds were good to eat—especially sheldrake. The two sisters, who loved to see the beautiful sheldrake in flight, were filled with dismay when they were brought in for dinner. But their brother was a masterful man and they had no redress. One day he shot a heron and insisted that it should be cooked.

> There was an iron hook in the central beam of the big vacant room he had spoken of, and on this hook he suspended the heron by its legs, its long pointed beak nearly touching the tiled floor, and hanging there with nothing else in the room it looked bigger than ever. It troubled them greatly to have to go through this room many times a day, but it was far worse at night. They were accustomed, especially on moonlight nights, to go that way to the dairy without a candle; and they sometimes forgot about the bird, and then the sight of it in its pale grey plumage would startle them as if they had seen a ghost. How awful it looked, with its wings like great arms half-open as if to scare them!

At last, after many weeks had gone by, the brother announced at breakfast one morning that the heron was in perfect cooking condition and they would have it that day for dinner. But, he added, it should not be the usual twelve o'clock meal: so important an occasion must be celebrated by a proper evening dinner at eight. 'Then he went out and left them staring into each other's pale face.' Eventually they got to work, somewhat deterred by finding a semi-decomposed trout nearly a foot long in the heron's gullet: but 'after refreshing themselves with sal-volatile and half-an-hour in the garden, they finished the hateful business by singeing it and pumping many gallons of water over its carcase, and then, towards evening, put it in the oven to roast or bake.' To please their brother they put the best silver on the table, and he was in an excellent temper:

> Then the heron on a big dish was brought in, and the brother rose to carve it, and heaped their plates with generous slices of the lean black flesh, and helped himself even more generously. They having been helped first had to begin, but to put even the smallest morsel into their mouths was more than they could do. They pretended to cut and eat it while confining themselves to the vegetables on their plates. Their brother was not affected with such squeamishness and straightway started operations, and did honour to the heron by taking a tremendous mouthful...

then rose and fled from the room. Next morning the sisters buried the remains of the bird in the garden.

Hudson could tell a story like this effectively because he never strained after the effect or attempted to force the humour. He allows it to emerge for itself, and the very economy and objectivity of his narrative heightens the absurdity. There are many such examples in his books, from the sly gaucho humour of *The Purple Land* to the story in the *Hind* of the deaf old lady who followed the preacher's movements with her ear-trumpet. As he moved about, now bending down, now on his toes, now leaning to the left, now wheeling to the right, the ear-trumpet would follow him, curling round in all directions and appearing above the pew 'like a crest.'

Humour proceeds from the incongruous. The effect of incongruity in a universe of order startles us out of our groove and results in a shock of mental liberation. I have spoken earlier on of Hudson's sense of the incongruous and his love for the strange. They are closely related; but while incongruity excites to humour, strangeness is sometimes akin to fear—as in the case of our reactions to the serpent, a creature to which, as we have seen, Hudson was continually attracted.

The serpent chapters in *The Book of a Naturalist* are among the best he ever wrote. They were part of a proposed 'Book of the Serpent,' often contemplated but never written. In the chapters entitled 'The Serpent's Strangeness' and 'The Bruised Serpent' he goes into the question of the place of reptiles in history, mythology, and literature, and discusses the psychological and religious origins of the common attitude towards them. In seeking to explain the distrust and fear with which the serpent is held, he observes that whether 'we believe with theologians that our great spiritual enemy was the real tempter, who merely made use of the serpent's form as a convenient disguise in which to approach the woman, or take without gloss the simple story as it stands in Genesis, which only says that the serpent was the most subtle of all things made and the cause of our undoing, the result for the creature is equally disastrous.' But this does not follow, since the serpent is used both in the Old and the New Testament as the symbol of Divine Love and Wisdom. The fiery serpent of the desert symbolized the Atonement, the act of perfect love, and Our Lord himself bade us be 'wise as serpents.' The fact is, as has been pointed out over and over again, the objects of symbolism are neutral in themselves and may be changed at will. No doubt the Genesis story has something to do with it, but more probably the cause of our revulsion is due to the serpent's strange mode of locomotion and its disagreeable effect on the nerves.

Hudson has some provocative things to say on the subject of dogs in this book, and his chapter, 'The Great Dog Superstition,' aroused violent controversy when it first appeared as an article in *Macmillan's Magazine*. The editor wrote to Hudson saying that the article had given him 'a painful shock,' and that it would 'hurt and disgust many readers of the Magazine'; and a lady whom Hudson greatly admired described him as 'worse than a vivisectionist'—which, he added, 'struck me as being a bit thick, seeing that a vivisectionist had always been to her the most damnable being in the universe.' Yet all he had done was to criticize dog-worship, and put forward the view that the dog is not superior, and in some ways inferior, in intelligence and affection to many other animals. He also drew attention to its dirty habits and love of foul smells—but this is common knowledge and should not have worried anybody. He suggested that we should break away from the monotony of the cat and dog, and attempt to tame other equally, or more, attractive creatures, for 'their hearts may also be conquered with kindness.' Doubtless he was over-sanguine; for experience has shown that a great length of time is necessary to make an animal breed tame. But there is something to be said for his suggestion, and the evidence he gives in a previous chapter on the effect of the Muzzling Act in improving the tempers of the dog population is revealing.

On the question of dog-worship I am entirely in agreement with Hudson. It seems to me that there is something essentially immoral in an exaggerated attachment to any animal, especially when, as so often, it goes with an attitude of indifference to or contempt for man. Thus the lady who was so angry with Hudson quoted 'certain sayings of Schopenhauer describing man as a very contemptible creature when compared with the dog. . . .' This is not surprising from Schopenhauer in view of his pessimistic philosophy, but it hardly does credit to his reasoning, since a few moments' reflection would have shown him that the notion of contemptibility is a human judgment and derives from the presence in man of values and ideals against which the contemptible is measured, and which set him far above any animal, domestic or otherwise. There is a certain type of neurotic egoist who cannot get on with his fellow men, but is excessively devoted to domestic animals, since they are not only inferior but often blindly worshipful, and can be dictated to without fear of contradiction. It was against this abnormal type that Hudson's criticism was directed, not against the ordinary animal or dog lover;

and the reactions of people to his article showed to which type they belonged. Unfortunately the dog has been the worst object of sentimental adulation, and Hudson singled him out for this reason. He had no feeling against dogs or any domestic animals; but the range of his affection for all living things was such that the adulation of domestic animals seemed to him unjustified, and often went with a complete insensitiveness to other creatures and to nature as a whole. His attitude to all non-human creatures, whether domestic or wild, was summed up in his own words: 'Neither pet nor persecute.' He observed dogs with sympathy and detachment, and the charming chapter, 'My Friend Jack,' with which *Afoot in England* concludes, shows that he could and did appreciate the canine qualities. Those who object to the dog chapters in *The Book of a Naturalist* should read 'My Friend Jack' if they want to get Hudson's views on dogs in perspective.

At first glance the life of a domestic animal seems to be a curious anomaly in the world, an exception to the universal law of suffering, so perfect is it by comparison with all other lives, human and non-human. Through no merit of its own, and by no part in the evolutionary scheme—indeed by nothing but sheer luck—a well-cared-for dog or cat goes through life with the minimum of mental and physical suffering: it passes its time in sleeping, eating, playing, and being fussed over until it dies or is put to sleep. Of course, this satisfaction may not be so perfect as we imagine: there is loss as well as gain, and domestication may bring with it an element of anxiety. In the words of Gerald Heard—'as far as we teach them our consciousness and strive to give them our security we must awake in them—as indeed it would seem we often do with some of our pets—a sense of anxiety, a sense of time. We are removing their natural protection, their blessed ignorance, their power of instantaneiety, letting the penumbra of time impinge on the bright flash of their eternity.' Self-consciousness is an evolutionary gain, but man is, in his present stage at any rate, imprisoned by it, whereas the animals, though lowlier in the plane of experience, enjoy life objectively in a series of presents that, in Heard's vivid phrase, are like bright flashes of eternity; and it was precisely the loss of this power that the extravert Hudson, himself living so intensely in the present, mourned in the domestic animal. The loss is still greater in the case of the utilitarian animals, such as the cow and the pig. Apart from the horse who is often treated as a pet, the majority of utilitarian animals have degenerated. The exaggeration of their purely functional and productive parts has brought about a condition which places them below both the 'self-conscious' domestic and the active wild animal. But Hudson could see possibilities even in such lowly creatures, and one of the best chapters in *The Book of a Naturalist* is entitled 'My Friend the Pig.' It is wholly delightful, and full of acute observation, humour, and charm.

The Book of a Naturalist was followed by the revised version of *Argentine Ornithology*, now entitled *Birds of La Plata*; and after this came *A Traveller in Little Things*, Hudson's last book of essays, save for the *Hind*, which stands somewhat apart. In the first essay of the *Traveller* he tells us how he found his title. One morning, in the coffee-room of a commercial hotel at Bristol, a very well-dressed and respectable old traveller with silvery white hair, gold-rimmed spectacles, and gold watch-chain, got into conversation with him and talked intelligently on a variety of subjects. Later, when Hudson began to talk about farming and agriculture, the old commercial listened with great interest and said that he saw that Hudson knew more than himself about such things and concluded that he did a very small line in the villages and country towns; that he was, in short, a 'traveller in little things.' For his own part, he added, he was a traveller in something very big that took him to great towns and cities. It is amusing to contrast the old commercial's idea of Hudson as a small-line traveller with the original and sensitive genius, already known as one of the greatest writers of English prose, who sat before him; yet I think there is something very charming and touching about this story when we realize how close to the truth he was. In his mind's eye, he saw his tall, gaunt, bearded companion with the high stiff collar (Hudson seems always to have worn this monstrosity) as a typical small-line traveller in little things who wandered about the country from village to village: and he was right. Hudson was a traveller in little things. A country-woman's smile, a bird's song, a shower of rain, a long-forgotten epitaph, the magpie chatter of gypsies, and the slow talk of shepherds—these were his line. But the little things he offers in this book are not, as a whole, among his best. He had done a better line elsewhere. The essays are very short, and come nearer than any in his previous books to the self-contained, complete essay we associate with the name of E. V. Lucas. There is no central theme as in the earlier essays, and we miss the sense of continuity that such a theme affords. Nevertheless, like all his later work, the *Traveller* is very mature. Many of the small sketches have great beauty, notably 'The Return of the Chiffchaff: (Spring Sadness),' one of the loveliest and most poignant things he ever wrote. Without a trace of sentimentality or of that morbid pessimism that so often mars the work of the sceptic and materialist, he conjures up the inexplicable sadness awakened by the impact of natural beauty in certain moods. Listening to the sweet insistent notes of the chiffchaff he falls to musing upon the long and perilous journey on which it has come, and there rises up before him the memory of springs that are gone and of friends long dead.

Is there no escape, then, from this intolerable sadness—from the thought of springs that have been, the beautiful multitudinous life that is vanished? Our maker and mother mocks at our efforts—at our philosophic refuges, and sweeps them away with a wave of emotion. And yet there is deliverance, the old way of escape which is ours, whether we want it or not. Nature herself in her own good time heals the wound she inflicts—even this most grievous in seeming when she takes away from us the faith and hope of reunion with our lost. They may be in a world of light, waiting our coming—we do not know; but in that place they are unimaginable, their state inconceivable. They were like us, beings of flesh and blood, or we should not have loved them. If we cannot grasp their hands their continued existence is nothing to us. Grief at their loss is just as great for those who have kept their faith as for those who have lost it; and on account of its very poignancy it cannot endure in either case. It fades, returning in its old intensity at ever longer intervals until it ceases. The poet of nature was wrong when he said that without his faith in the decay of his senses he would be worse than dead, echoing the apostle who said that if we had hope in this world only we should be of all men the most miserable. So, too, was the later poet wrong when he listened to the waves on Dover beach bringing the eternal note of sadness in; when he saw in imagination the ebbing of the great sea of faith which had made the world so beautiful, in its withdrawal disclosing the deserts drear and naked shingles of the world. That desolation, as he imagined it, which made him so unutterably sad, was due to the erroneous idea that our earthly happiness comes to us from otherwhere, some region outside our planet, just as one of our modern philosophers has imagined that the principle of life on earth came originally from the stars.

The 'naked shingles of the world' is but a mood of our transitional day; the world is just as beautiful as ever it was, and our dead as much to us as they have been, even when faith was at its highest. They are not wholly, irretrievably lost, even when we cease to remember them, when their images come no longer unbidden to our minds. They are present in nature: through ourselves, receiving but what we give, they have become part and parcel of it and give it an expression. As when the rain clouds disperse and the sun shines out once more, heaven and earth are filled with a chastened light, sweet to behold and very wonderful, so because of our lost ones, because of the old grief at their loss, the visible world is touched with a new light, a tenderness and grace and beauty not its own.

Once again the old problem of death and immortality;

but in this passage Hudson falls back upon the unsatisfactory answer that we are merged in nature—an answer that temporarily satisfies the emotions while intellectually leaving the problem exactly where it was before. Never did he solve the conflict between his love of life and doubt of survival, albeit the recurrence of the theme in so many of his finest passages shows that the spark of inspiration was continually struck off from the conflict. In the above quotation he speaks of our maker and mother sweeping away our philosophic refuges 'with a wave of emotion'; and it is true that doubt is very often emotional in contrast with 'our philosophic refuges' which more frequently involve the higher powers of reason and will. But it is not, as Hudson would persuade us, nature who sweeps away our beliefs with a wave of emotion. It is the irrational principle of negation in ourselves. Neither is it true to say that grief for the departed is as great in those who have kept their faith as in those who have lost it. Both believer and unbeliever alike experience grief at the loss of something loved; but the experience of the believer is tempered by a rational hope. As Berdyaev has put it, we cannot get rid of suffering but we can understand it. Understanding brings into being a value that transcends, though it does not intrinsically lessen, suffering. The value that Hudson found in nature was not the supreme value of understanding that proceeds from the message of the Cross, but it served, in its field of aesthetic intuition, to ward off the horrors of atheistic despair. The note of serenity with which the passage ends is a witness to Hudson's faith.

At the conclusion of his book our traveller offers us a sample of verse. It is slight and undistinguished; for like so many men who displayed great sensibility and power in prose, Hudson was surprisingly limited in the poetic field. The poem, part of which I quote below, appeared in the *Selborne Magazine* in 1897, though why it was resurrected in a book written twenty-four years later is hard to say:

It must be true, I 've sometimes thought,
That beings from some realm afar
Oft wander in the void immense,
Flying from star to star.

In silence through this various world,
They pass, to mortal eyes unseen,
And toiling men in towns know not
That one with them has been.

But oft, when on the woodland falls
A sudden hush, and no bird sings;
When leaves, scarce fluttered by the wind,
Speak low of sacred things,

My heart has told me I should know,
In such a lonely place, if one
From other worlds came there and stood
Between me and the sun.

Hudson's essays, as a whole, reveal an extraordinary variety; there is scarcely any part of life he has failed to touch, and touching, to make new with the power of his genius. Passion, humour, pathos, tragedy, fantasy, irony, characterization, description—all are there. Many have been dissuaded from reading him on account of his being labelled a naturalist, believing him to be limited accordingly; but a glance at one of the least distinguished of his essays should be sufficient to dispel that illusion.

THE AUTOBIOGRAPHY

One of the chief fruits of the Romantic Movement, whether for good or ill, was an increase of subjectivism in literature and the arts. In literature it found expression in the autobiographical form, of which Rousseau, the prophet of romanticism, was so great a master. But although, since Rousseau, the autobiographical form has become increasingly popular, there have been very few good autobiographies, owing to the extreme rareness of any genuine talent for this kind of writing. The difficulties, both of conception and expression, are very great. Good autobiography must be neither too personal nor too objective. If too personal it will tend to be amorphous, and fail to make adequate contact with the reader: if too objective it will lose its intimate character and degenerate into mere reporting. Although the writer's personality should never be lost sight of, it must, at the same time, be framed by the objective events of his narrative within which it has developed. This rule, it seems to me, applies to all autobiographical writing, whether analytical and introspective, or descriptive. Some autobiographers lay the main emphasis upon their reactions to events; others emphasize the events, and are more interested in what happened than in how they reacted. Both may write successful autobiography; but neither can afford to ignore the subtle relation between the personal and the objective.

Hudson, on account of the variety and balance of his mind, was supremely fitted for the task. He was sensitive and imaginative, and at the same time vividly aware of the outer world. He combined insight with interest to a remarkable degree, and his work, though always informed by his unique personality, was objective in intent. He was personal without being an egoist: objective without being shallow. Above all, he possessed an extraordinary memory which enabled him to re-create and relive the past. If to these gifts we add the background of his full and happy life and the circumstances in which his Autobiography came to be written we shall see how propitious the moment was for the production of a masterpiece. In a sense, all his work is autobiographical; but it is, for the most part, made up of odds and ends and bits of his experience. The Autobiography gives us a planned and continuous narrative up to about his eighteenth year.

When Hudson wrote *Far Away and Long Ago* he was nearing the end of a long life of unusually rich experience. He was also at the height of his literary powers. The impulse came to him at exactly the right moment, and he was able to write in surroundings that gave him perfect quiet and repose. He was ill, and was being looked after in a convent hospital on the south coast—a place which, in Roberts's words, 'he often remembered gratefully'; and while he lay there a great flood of memories came back to him, the process of which he describes in the opening of the book:

I was feeling weak and depressed when I came down from London one November evening to the south coast; the sea, the clear sky, the bright colours of the afterglow kept me too long on the front in an east wind in that low condition, with the result that I was laid up for six weeks with a very serious illness. Yet when it was over I looked back on those six weeks as a happy time! Never had I thought so little of physical pain. Never had I felt confinement less—I who feel, when I am out of sight of living, growing grass, and out of sound of bird's voices and all rural sounds, that I am not properly alive!

On the second day of my illness, during an interval of comparative ease, I fell into recollections of my childhood, and at once I had that far, that forgotten past with me again as I had never previously had it. It was not like that mental condition, known to most persons, when some sight or sound or, more frequently, the perfume of some flower, associated with our early life, restores the past suddenly and so vividly that it is almost an illusion. That is an intensely emotional condition and vanishes as quickly as it comes. This was different. To return to the simile and metaphor used at the beginning, it was as if the cloud shadows and haze had passed away and the entire wide prospect beneath me made clearly visible. Over it all my eyes could range at will, choosing this or that point to dwell upon, to examine it in all its details; or in the case of some person known to me as a child, to follow his life till it ended or passed from sight; then to return to the same point again to repeat the process with other lives and resume my rambles in the old familiar haunts.

What a happiness it would be, I thought, in spite of discomfort and pain and danger, if this vision would continue! It was not to be expected: nevertheless it did not vanish, and on the second day I set myself to try and save it from the oblivion which would presently cover it again. Propped up with pillows I began with pencil and writing-pad to put it down in some sort of order, and went on with it at intervals during the whole six weeks of my confinement, and in this way produced the first rough draft of the book.

And all this time I never ceased wondering at my own mental state; I thought of it when, quickly tired, my trembling fingers dropped the pencil; or when I woke from uneasy sleep to find the vision still before me, inviting, insistently calling to me, to resume my childish rambles and adventures of long ago in that strange world where I first saw the light.

It was to me a marvellous experience; to be here, propped up with pillows in a dimly lighted room, the night-nurse idly dozing by the fire; the sound of the everlasting wind in my ears, howling outside and dashing the rain like hailstones against the window panes; to be awake to all this, feverish and ill and sore, conscious of my danger too, and at the same time to be thousands of miles away, out in the sun and wind, rejoicing in other sights and sounds, happy again with that ancient long-lost and now recovered happiness!

The extraordinary uprush of memory of which he speaks may have been partly due to his illness—probably the old heart trouble complicated by other factors. Every one knows the peculiar mental and physical reactions produced by disturbances of the heart, and if to this we add the further disturbances produced by feverishness and high temperature, during which the forces of the unconscious are released, we can easily see how it was that Hudson should be in such an abnormally sensitive and potent condition. At the same time he was at the height of his creative power, and the control which this power imparted to the exuberance of his memory and the intensity of his inspiration gave us a masterpiece. For the next three years he worked at the book, slowly, carefully, as was his wont, bringing to perfection that first rough draft and shaping it into one of the greatest autobiographies in the language. Frank Swinnerton says that the book was influenced by Aksakoff's *History of my Childhood*. It may be so; but I find it hard to believe that a thing so uniquely and maturely Hudson owes much to any other writer.

Like *A Shepherd's Life*, the Autobiography glows with the light of memory; but it lacks the perfect serenity of the earlier work which, as we saw, derived its unique quality from the enshrinement of memory at one remove—the shepherd's memories remembered again by Hudson. In *Far Away and Long Ago* the memories are direct and personal, and their impact is more emotionally charged, more vivid, more immediate. I have spoken earlier of Hudson's realism and power of living in the present, and it was this vivid experience of the present that enabled him to bring so rich a store from the past. Because each present experience was completely enjoyed it left a lasting impression on the memory.

Great happiness and great pain leave the deepest impressions on the memory; but in many cases the emotional content of pain is transformed by the past and made pleasurable. By separating us from the immediate contact of pain memory has a similar effect to that of tragedy wherein we enter into and sympathize with a painful situation while in the act of enjoying it. Past suffering is painful only when it forces itself upon us, as in great grief. When it is selected by the memory in tranquillity it becomes pleasurable. In this, the recollection of the past is related to dreams, which, apart from the special case of terror dreams, are pervaded by tranquillity. Events which in waking life are painful do not hurt us in dreams. As J. W. Dunne has reminded us, dreams are usually very lovely things; and no dream is ever boring. A boring dream is an impossibility because we are released from the self-consciousness of time—as we are also, in a more controlled degree, when we recollect the past. Wordsworth's definition of poetry as 'emotion recollected in tranquillity,' may be one-sided, but it does perfectly describe the dream-like quality of much of the best poetry and literature. The very title of Hudson's Autobiography has the quality of distance and remoteness. The attraction of distance both in space and time is universal, and may derive from the sense of exile that is common to us all. Certainly there is no lovelier or more poignant experience than journeying towards green places far away, or going back across the fields of memory to events long past. For the past is the strangest of all human modes of experience. It is that which exists in no longer existing. The present is, and the future is not; but the past both is and is not—hence its mystery and charm, and its fatal fascination for those who despair of life. But whereas the pessimist is imprisoned within the ivory tower of the past, the realist, such as Hudson, is the tenant of the tower and occupies it at will.

Hudson was under no illusions as to the past, and the story he tells in *Far Away and Long Ago* is not without its dark side. But it is, on the whole, the story of an exceptionally happy childhood. It is possible to attribute to our childhood a happiness that was not, at the time, genuine; and it is equally possible, as the moderns have shown, to describe childhood in terms of a morbid psychology that is no less unreal. It all depends upon the temperament and selective power of the author. Neither ideal nor morbid is a proper term to apply to average childhood, but the former is nearer the truth in most cases.

There seems little doubt that Hudson's childhood

approximated very closely to the ideal. He was blest with the three things essential to a normal development: good parents, a happy home, and the presence of nature. It is often pointed out how restless is the modern child compared with the child of previous generations; and one of the chief reasons given is the instability of the contemporary world—the break-up of values, the perpetual menace of revolution and war. Now while it is true that, as Adler has emphasized, no child can grow into a normal adult with a full sense of his responsibilities if he is continually haunted by the fear of insecurity, I would suggest that there is another inhibiting force greater than, or at least as great as, insecurity. Modern industrial life, even when secure, cuts off the child from nature with its eternal recurrence and renewal so essential as a background to the growth of character, and produces a sense of impersonality accompanied by a ceaseless intrusion of noise, rush, and mechanization. Up to a hundred years ago the majority of children were reared in a hamlet or village or small country town with a stable background of agricultural life and the rhythm of the seasons. Against this, external instability and even catastrophe seldom made a permanent effect on the character, since the presence of nature brought with it an intuitive feeling that there was something larger and more enduring than any human change. As a result, the generations that grew up in those days, though perhaps in some ways less sensitive, were hardier and better balanced than ourselves. Hudson's own childhood illustrates the relative insignificance of human catastrophe against the background of nature, for it was spent among a barbarous people who enjoyed nothing so much as banditry, revolution, and war. Always the distant rumble of one or other of these national diversions reached them from the big towns, and sometimes bands of desperate men would come to the house. The gauchos, though charming and picturesque in many ways, were violent-tempered, and every man was an artist in the use of the knife. Here, then, was an environment by no means secure; but nature was the stabilizing force, and it was nature that moulded Hudson's childhood and gave it serenity in spite of revolution and war.

The gauchos whom we met in *The Purple Land* come to life more vividly in the mature pages of the Autobiography, which contains many unforgettable sketches of this strange people, and some of the most perfect human portraits Hudson ever drew. It also contains some of his finest writing on nature. The interplay of human and wild life which exists in all his books is never better done than here, perhaps because, in that wild country, the gulf between them was relatively small.

Apart from the gauchos, many strange characters crossed the Hudsons' life from the outer world. There was the schoolmaster, Mr. Trigg, 'an Englishman, a short, stoutish, almost fat little man, with grey hair, clean-shaved sunburnt face, a crooked nose which had been broken or was born so, clever mobile mouth, and blue-grey eyes with a humourous twinkle in them and crow's-feet at the corners.' He had been an actor in his youth, and would read Dickens aloud, impersonating the characters with zest. He got on very well with adults, but was too much of a tyrant to inspire affection in children, and at last was forced to leave the house for striking them in a violent temper. 'It was an unspeakable relief,' says Hudson, looking back over sixty years, 'a joyful moment; yet on that very day, and on the next before he rode away, I, even I who had been unjustly and cruelly struck with a horsewhip, felt my little heart heavy in me when I saw the change in his face—the dark, still, brooding look, and knew that the thought of his fall and the loss of his home was exceedingly bitter to him.' The new schoolmaster was Father O'Keefe, 'an Irish priest without a cure and with nothing to do.' He was a gentle, absent-minded man, very fond of fishing and not very strict or effective as a teacher. The children devised a game with him when he was out riding absorbed in his own thoughts: 'we would dash forward with a shout, and when about forty yards from him we would all hurl our lances so as to make them fall just at the feet of his horse'; but never once did he notice anything. At last one day he remarked casually that he was going somewhere to visit someone and was seen no more.

It is remarkable how vividly we remember the 'characters' of our childhood—eccentric relatives, shopkeepers, schoolmasters, clergymen, and those curious beings who day after day we passed in lane or street, the tramps, gypsies, rag-and-bone men, and the rest. The uninhibited imagination of childhood seizes upon anything quaint or individual in the monotony of adult life, and later, when we look back, the 'characters' of those far-off days stand out sharp and clear with an almost divine quality. The majority of Dickens's characters are drawn from his childhood experiences—so also are many of the characters Hudson created in the Romances and re-created in the Essays and Autobiography.

I have spoken more than once of Hudson's feeling for serpents: it went back very far into childhood, and in this book he tells us of its origin. At first he took their bad reputation for granted, and was afraid of them and persecuted them like the rest of the household. Serpents were common in that part of the world, and there were seven or eight different kinds. He tells us how a colony made themselves at home in the foundations of the house. 'In winter they hibernated there, tangled together in a cluster no doubt; and in summer nights, when they were at home, coiled at their ease or gliding ghost-like about their subterranean apartments, I would lie awake and listen to them by the hour'—and he goes on to describe the extraordinary variety of their 'hissing conversations.' Here was the first awakening of that mixed emotion of fascination and repulsion which serpents evoke. Later he speaks of the pleasure of finding the cast-off slough of a serpent's skin, which gave him a feeling of relief that he could handle its likeness without fear. Then came the incident of the lady who rescued a serpent from a man who was about to kill it, and the adventure with a strange serpent, black and mysterious, who lived in a dry, sun-baked, weedy piece of ground that he watched with fear and excitement for many days. Gradually interest and affection came to supplant fear, and we have, as a result, the unique serpent chapters in *The Book of a Naturalist*.

In those days, before the coming of civilization, the pampas must have been a paradise for a child in love with nature. It was a land of surpassing richness and abundance of life, a land of storm and sun and illimitable horizons, and always the sound of wings and the cries of many birds together. Here was nourished that deep understanding and devotion which set Hudson's writings on birds apart from all others. Chief among the great birds of that ancient world were the flamingoes.

At last we came out to a smooth grass turf, and in a little while were by the stream, which had overflowed its banks owing to recent heavy rains and was now about fifty yards wide. An astonishing number of birds were visible—chiefly wild duck, a few swans, and many waders—ibises, herons, spoonbills, and others, but the most wonderful of all were three immensely tall white-and-rose-coloured birds, wading solemnly in a row a yard or so apart from one another some twenty yards out from the bank. I was amazed and enchanted at the sight, and my delight was intensified when the leading bird stood still and, raising his head and long neck aloft, opened and shook his wings. For the wings when open were of a glorious crimson colour, and the bird was to me the most angel-like creature on earth.

These were the birds, described at the end of *El Ombú*, so eagerly watched for by poor Monica, who cried out with delight every time a flock went by. The plain was full of stately birds, and here Hudson grew familiar with the kind of avian life that is denied to those living in more civilized lands, the life of great birds in the mass, in which the majesty and the beauty of nature are most perfectly related.

'What more did I want?' he asks. What more, indeed, with this marvellous fecundity of nature always at hand. He accepted it thankfully and joyfully, retaining the joy of it all his life; and long afterwards, in the imperishable pages of the Autobiography the emotion was recaptured and communicated, and we rejoice with him and live our childhood over again. The pervading quality of the book is a simple, emotional acceptance of life, the continual sense of wonder of the child. Many artists, and perhaps all naturists, retain something of the child's vision—the naïve element of delight in the simple, sensuous, and direct; and much of the attraction of Hudson is his retention of a childlike acceptance in a mature and adult mind. In the Autobiography the two sides of him are revealed in perfect fusion: the mature old man, with his long and varied experience of life, looks back at his childhood; and the two, the old self and the young, are, by some mysterious alchemy, one. Always he retained the childlike sense of wonder and delight in the visible world. Many of us have lost this quality, not because it has been replaced by something higher, but because it has disintegrated into something lower. It has been said that, compared with adults, children—within the limits of childhood—are relatively integrated; and it is true that all children, even the spoiled and wretched, have a quality of wholeness that is, in most cases, lacking in adult life. The expansion of the ego and the development of reason lead to bewilderment, and give rise to the conflicts that produce disintegration. That which integrates, in both child and adult, is faith and devotion. In the child it is a simple faith expressing itself in devotion to little things: in the adult it is a deeper faith relating to objects of ultimate value; but no matter how different in degree, it is the same quality of faith and devotion that integrates.

As Hudson matured, his childhood delight in the visible world increased, reaching its culmination in the second childhood of old age. Second childhood usually means failure of the faculties; but where the mind is alert it is a state to be envied. As Miss Elizabeth Myers put it in discussing J. C. Powys's *The Art of Growing Old*, old age 'is the ideal time *consciously* to practise what we *unconsciously* indulged in our cradles—a packed and shameless enjoyment of our simplest, commonest sensations, increasing those moments which, as Santayana would say, are "each a dramatic perspective of the world," and bringing us close to the secret of the universe.' All his life Hudson was close to the heart of that secret: his 'simplest, commonest sensations' were not merely enjoyed, but *lived* with a conscious intensity in his imagination, and continually overflowed in the creativity of his writing. No one knew better the art of growing old, and no one ever had a gift more perfectly fitted to express it. Here, at the very end, we see him, tired and ill and lonely, recapturing the happiness of his childhood across a span of seventy years.

Not that his childhood was all happiness. The gnawing doubt of immortality and 'the murmur of the far-off battle of evolution' troubled him. In 'A Darkened Life,' one of the most moving chapters in the book, he tells of doubt and illness and the stopping up of the creative channels of his imagination. We have seen many examples of his continual preoccupation with the problem of life after death, and here he tells us how it first came to him—through some chance words of Mr. Trigg the schoolmaster. An old dog, Caesar, had died and had been buried by Mr. Trigg. When the ceremony was over he 'looked round at us and said solemnly: 'That 's the end. Every dog has his day and so has every man; and the end is the same for both. We die like old Caesar, and are put into the ground and have the earth shovelled over us.' These simple words affected Hudson more than any he had ever heard—'They pierced me to the heart'; and from that time until the end of his life the wound remained. Sometimes, in conversation with Roberts, he would irritably deny that he had any belief in immortality; but it haunted him always—the thought of 'all the beauty that is vanished and returneth not.' When, in adolescence, this problem was most acute, it was complicated by the serious illness which permanently affected his heart, and the result seems to have been a kind of night of the senses, a recession of immediate, sensuous reality, a withdrawal, not so much of God in Himself as of His presence in nature as Hudson dimly apprehended it.

But in the next, and final, chapter he tells us how he found integration once more, and emerged from his dark night never again to lose faith in life. Though he lived continually in the shadow of death as a result of the damage to his heart, and though he was often troubled by the shadows of doubt and despair, always the serene and affirmative note sounds through his work, and never with more insistence than in the Autobiography, which closes with these words:

> Thus I came out of the contest a loser, but as a compensation had the knowledge that my physicians were false prophets; that, barring accidents, I could count on thirty, forty, even fifty years with their summers and autumns and winters. And that was the life I desired—the life the heart can conceive—the earth life. When I hear people say they have not found the world, and life so agreeable or interesting as to be in love with it, or that they look with equanimity to its end, I am apt to think they have never been properly alive nor seen with clear vision the world they think so meanly of, or anything in it—not a blade of grass. Only I know that mine is an exceptional case, that the visible world is to me more beautiful and interesting than to most persons, that the delight I experienced in my communings with Nature did not pass away, leaving nothing but a recollection of vanished happiness to intensify a present pain. The happiness was never lost, but owing to that faculty I have spoken of, had a cumulative effect on the mind and was mine again, so that in my worst times, when I was compelled to exist shut out from Nature in London for long periods, sick and poor and friendless, I could yet always feel that it was infinitely better to be than not to be.

THE LAST TESTAMENT

HUDSON'S last book, *A Hind in Richmond Park*, written in his eighty-second year, is an astonishing achievement, youthful in spirit, vigorous in thought, original in conception. Though not his most perfect work—*A Shepherd's Life* and the Autobiography are more aesthetically satisfying—it is certainly the most powerful and compelling book he ever wrote. At a time when most men are verging upon senility he was discovering new paths. I know of no other parallel to his achievement unless it be Bridges's *Testament of Beauty*, completed at eighty-four, or the last great operas of Verdi's old age, *Othello* and *Falstaff*. The two operas have some resemblance in character to the Autobiography and the *Hind*; the rich splendour and maturity of *Othello* in the first, the youthful vigour and branching into new paths of *Falstaff* in the second. But Hudson's achievement was, I think, even more remarkable than that of Bridges and Verdi on account of his ill health. He was ill when he wrote the Autobiography, and he was ill, intermittently, during the writing of the *Hind*. A few years before, John Pardoe, the heart surgeon, had declared his heart to be 'awful rubbish.' The strain of creative work was too much for him, and he died before he could make the final revision of the concluding pages of the *Hind*. It was left to Roberts to arrange the material as best he could from an almost illegible manuscript; and without altering a word, he succeeded in giving us the nearest thing possible to Hudson's final intentions. As I point out in the preface, the Autobiography and the *Hind* are the closest approximation to an explicit statement of Hudson's outlook: the Autobiography gives the origins of that which the *Hind* reveals in its full and final expression. But it was final only through his death, for if he had lived he would certainly have taken us further.

Unlike the spacious Autobiography, which is the kind of work we should expect from serene old age, the *Hind* startles and challenges by its vigour. The title gives no indication of the scope and richness of the contents; but though, in a sense, it is misleading, it does give a clue to the book, and is attractive in its elusiveness. Hudson is concerned mainly with the senses in animals and man, and with imaginative sensibility, the 'spiritualizing' element that in man raises the life of the senses to a higher plane. Although, as I have said, it is the nearest we ever get to an explicit statement of Hudson's beliefs, the light still falls obliquely, and there is nowhere any attempt at an ordered philosophy of nature. But it is the brightest of all the rainbow colours of his vision, and is more revealing than any philosophy of nature, however closely reasoned or eloquently argued. Hudson is the artist and the seer still; but in the *Hind* we come nearer to his full meaning than elsewhere. It contains and sums up aspects of everything he had previously written. Autobiography, anecdote, literary criticism, topography, natural history, speculations on biology, psychology, art, and religion—all are surveyed over a broad field of time and space, and perpetually illumined by his unique personality at its most mature. It is the apotheosis of the free, discursive, yet organic essay form he made his own, though it is not, like many of the previous essays, a mere collection of material, but a continuous whole growing freely from a small and insignificant beginning. At the age of eighty-one Hudson was groping towards a new form of expression that included but surpassed the old.

In writing this book I am occasionally reminded of a mushroom-gathering experience on some warm misty September morning when my eyes were searching the ground about or before me while my mind was occupied with some other matter. Here, at this spot, I find no fewer than three perfect beauties—silvery-white hemispherical bosses in the green carpet, and, gathering them, I go on delighted at my success. Then, after going thirty yards or so, I all at once remember that on first sighting them I had distinctly counted four mushrooms and am compelled to retrace my steps to try and re-find the one I had left ungathered. So with the book: from time to time a something omitted comes back and obliges me to break off and go some distance back, if not to the starting point.

I may be told that I am to blame in not having mapped out my route beforehand, and that the only thing to do now is to break up the work and build it afresh. It would not suit me to do that.

No doubt any one who had got as far as the second chapter has formed the idea that this is to be a mere collection of incidents and impressions, with comments thereon, on a great variety of subjects—a book without a plan, a sort of *olla podrida*. It is not so. When I first observed the hind in Richmond Park my thought was about its senses, which led me to compare them with those of other animals, including man; and as I possessed a store of my own observations on the subject, supplemented with others from reading, I foresaw when I began to set them down that a book would result. It then occurred to me that in this work I would not follow the usual method by setting down the heads or leading themes in their proper order, then working them out. My own unmethodical method would be to let the observation and the thought carry me whithersoever it would.

We know from Butler, if not from our own feeble efforts at making poetry, that rhymes the rudders are of verses by which they often steer their courses;—a queer sort of rudder with a mind of its own to carry us into places which we had no intention of visiting! But it is quite true; and so with this rudder of mine which takes me where it will, and if it overshoots the mark and goes back I must go back with it. My plan then is an unplanned one, a picking up as I go along of a variety of questions concerning the senses, just as they rise spontaneously from what has gone before.

Having got thus far with my explanations I must now throw over the mushroom-gathering simile, seeing that the business I am occupied with is more of the nature of tree-climbing. The root thereof is the hind, her senses and behaviour, and from this root spring the trunk and branches I am climbing; and the trouble is that when I have finished exploring the branch I happened to be on and am about to proceed to the next one above it, I discover that I have left one beneath me unexplored and am obliged to return to it.

To my mind, neither mushroom-gathering nor tree-climbing is an adequate simile of the form and scope of the book. Hudson is, of course, speaking of himself as author and trying to explain his own method of work; but to an outsider the book has more the effect of a river, beginning as a little stream, and gradually, through many channels and tributaries, becoming a deep, full torrent, flowing towards the infinite sea of nature. The stream rises, simply, with an anecdote about a child and a hind in Richmond Park. At this point we are given no clue to what is to come, and there is nothing to distinguish the book from any other Hudson essay; but when he sits down to watch a hind 'with her trumpet ears,' observing how they move to catch the sounds coming from different directions and reflecting on the shape of the outer ear, the stream slowly begins to gather force: ears lead to sound, sound to the noise and effect of the wind, the effect of the wind to sense of smell, sense of smell to sense of direction, sense of direction to migration—all gathering impetus from many sources which come together in the full-flowing torrent of the last great chapters dealing with speech, sound, music, imagination, nature, art, and life, and a hundred things more.

In the final chapter Hudson's theme is the transcendence of art by nature. Unlike Shaw he did not believe that it would be transcended by thought and will, but only by something akin to, though greater than, itself—namely the imagination working upon the material which nature offers through the life of the senses. The increased sensibility imparted by man's 'spiritual' and imaginative powers is, for Hudson, the means by which he enters into the full life of nature, a life wherein all the partial aspects of sensibility that art enshrines are brought to completion.

In *Back to Methuselah* Shaw argues that art will become the plaything of children: imagination will be the servant of reason, not of sensibility, and reason will be driven by will. For Shaw, the life force 'needs a brain' for its fulfilment: for Hudson, nature needs the mirror of man's sensibility in which her beauty may be reflected and become conscious in him. Shaw is much influenced by Schopenhauer and Nietzsche, the philosophers of will, and on the subject of beauty he is inclined to be scornful. Tanner, the hero of *Man and Superman*, contends that life 'has not measured the success of its attempts at godhead by the beauty or bodily perfection of the result, since in both these respects the birds, as our friend Aristophanes long ago pointed out, are so extraordinarily superior, with their power of flight and their lovely plumage, and, may I add, the touching poetry of their loves and nestings, that it is inconceivable that Life, having once produced them, should, if love and beauty were her object, start off on another line and labour at the clumsy elephant and hideous ape, whose grandchildren we are.' No, Tanner adds, I sing 'the philosophic man: he who seeks in contemplation to discover the inner will of the world, in invention to discover the means of fulfilling that will, and in action to do that will by the so-discovered means.' Thus Shaw sees the supplanting of art through the apotheosis of world reason in the service of world will, while Hudson sees the transcendence of art in the contemplation of nature. Shaw's example of the elephants and apes as an argument against beauty as the final goal of life would have been used for exactly the opposite reason by Hudson to show the degeneration of such creatures from the vision implicit in the bird. Within his limits Hudson is nearer the truth; for if you are going to substitute for God the inadequate values of the life force and nature, the latter will, at least, give you something substantial to live for. The life force is an illogical conception, whereas nature is a living reality in which all men are rooted and from which they can draw sustenance. As S. Sagar has pointed out, all the modern attempts to go beyond nature and to deify will are futile and can lead to nothing but strife. In practice, the concept of ultimate will tends to manifest itself in the power of dictators. It is interesting to contrast Shaw's conception of Utopia in the final play of *Back to Methuselah* with that of Hudson in *A Crystal Age*. In each, sexuality has been transcended; but Shaw's Utopians manage somehow to develop life in a kind of artificial egg, while Hudson's are perpetuated in the person of the mother. After a brief period of adolescence, Shaw's Utopians live only to think, whereas Hudson's community is directed towards a life of sublimated sensibility. Shaw's Utopia could exist only in the remote future: Hudson's is, to some extent, a return to the past. He would recall us from this mechanical industrial world back to the life of earth, a life so beautiful that beside it all sexuality is feeble and all art inadequate.

As to how art is to be transcended in nature the *Hind* gives no clue, and the answer Hudson might have given he carried to the grave. He believed that art would pass; but he did not emulate his favourite novelist, Tolstoy, and renounce it—indeed he saw it as the only hope for man in his present state of development. He was, however, convinced that a full life of the sublimated senses in harmony with nature would ultimately render it obsolete. In the penultimate paragraph of the *Hind* he expresses the dissatisfaction with art we all feel at times:

> We see that this question of art is in a perpetual state of flux. To go back to the last century: we find that Ruskin was regarded as one of the higher critics of art, and that now his teaching is almost universally rejected; that his theory is all wrong for the young men. We also see that there is a revolt of a host of young artists against the art of all who came before them. We see groups in rebellion against what they call conventional art: the very art one knows in fact. These outbursts occur from time to time and tend to grow more frequent. In a little while they die

out, and the generation that follows laughs at their folly. But again, others spring up to take their place. Looking back, we see they do not and cannot lift art to a high plane. We see that art cannot progress; that on these lines and in that particular direction it reached its highest level ages ago. But the only explanation of these futile attempts is the sense of dissatisfaction with art generally, which every individual, young or old, with an alert progressive mind comes to in his own life. The revolt against 'conventional art,' even when it results in something we laugh at, is a sign of progress towards something above the arts, which will satisfy the creative powers, the desire of self-expression.

There is much truth in Hudson's contention that the modern aesthetic revolt is an attempt to go beyond art. Whatever may be the case with the other arts it certainly seems true of music. It is by no means improbable that music may have reached a dead end, whether temporary or permanent one cannot say. Any one at all familiar with modern music, in which every device of novelty has been exploited in melody, harmony, rhythm, and orchestral colour, will understand what I mean. In the most advanced music, the attempt of which Hudson speaks to 'progress towards something above the arts' is painfully obvious. The atonal Viennese school may be musically barren (with the one notable exception of Alban Berg's opera *Wozzeck*), but it can be understood—with other similar movements—as an attempt to go beyond art. I would observe, however, that although this modern tendency, which is found in all the arts to some extent, points to a transcendence of art, it is a transcendence more in the direction of the intellectual ultimate of Shaw than of the naturistic ultimate of Hudson.

The problem with which Hudson was faced, and which he did not attempt to answer, is this: If we reject thought as the final goal, what is going to satisfy the *creative* powers when art goes? for if art is transcended in nature, creativity must disappear and man be reduced to pure aesthetic contemplation. It is clear that Hudson did not regard this as desirable. He himself was in the peculiar position of having little need for art, and of finding his supreme joy in the contemplation of nature, while his creative impulse was satisfied through a literary medium that was a half-way house between sensibility and thought. Doubtless, with that breadth of mind which lay underneath all his 'salty prejudices,' he would have appreciated the position expressed by Herbert Read, who argues that nature does not transcend, but is the touchstone of art, and that while art must survive as long as humanity exists it will develop only so far as it is united to nature. A reviewer of one of Read's books summed up the position when he said that 'that which is common to all works of art is form, by form meaning the shape taken by the work as a whole; and the only touchstone of quality in form is nature, but by nature Mr. Read means "the whole organic process of life and movement which goes on in the universe." Truth to nature, in art, then, is truth to what are called the laws of nature, but this truth is not dependent on understanding them intellectually. They are sensed intuitively.' These are wise words; and whatever Hudson may have thought about the future of art they express very happily the quality of his sentiments about art in its present state.

Hudson calls the *Hind* 'a story without an end'; and so it is in the sense that the vision within it, as in all his works, is never complete. Its riches are inexhaustible. It offers us no clear-cut philosophy, no panacea; but when the light of Hudson's inspiration is upon us we have something much more than a philosophy; we have a refreshment of the spirit. Like the effect of clear air and sunlight on the body, his writings bring with them a quality of mental health in which each reader enriches his own philosophy of life. The sharing of Hudson's experience ennobles the mind far more than the panaceas of our economists, psychologists, and educationalists.

The message that emerges from the *Hind*, and the message of Hudson's whole life, is well summed up in some words of another great lover of nature, the Earl of Portsmouth. We must 'seek adjustment in humility with nature; of our own natures, the soil's nature, the nature of each growing life therein, and with that wider and still half-guessed harmony of all things which we call God.' Hudson sought and found 'adjustment in humility with nature.' It was not the transcendent humility of the saint, but it sprang from the same source—a single-hearted devotion. Hudson's devotion to nature was his religion, a giving of himself to what he genuinely believed to be the ultimate value; and the words of the above quotation seem to me to get as near as possible to what he felt when, in rare moments of illumination, he heard, afar off, the music of that 'harmony of all things which we call God.'

Although the *Hind* is so rich in thought and sensibility and comes so near to being a comprehensive summary of Hudson's beliefs, it is surprisingly deficient on the subject of religion. It is possible that in his next book he would have revised and completed the speculations on art with which the *Hind* ends, and have given us an outline of his religious outlook. He seems to have believed that, like art, organized, dogmatic religion would pass away; but the spirit of art and the spirit of religion—the sense of beauty, and the sense of the *numinous* expressed in awe and worship—would remain, since they are an essential part of life. He advocated a spiritualized or sublimated life of the senses as the basis of both the aesthetic and religious impulses, and unwittingly, though with an entirely different background and for very different reasons, took the line of Freud that the grosser impulses can be transcended by sublimating them into channels of creative imagination. But Freud (Hudson persisted in calling him 'Frood') reduced all impulses and the entire life of the senses to sexuality—a position which for Hudson was sheer nonsense, making, as he put it, 'the sex feeling *the* root instead of making it one of the many distinct elements contained in the root.' He believed that the root itself—that is, the whole of human personality—must take sustenance from the living soil of the earth; but at the same time he recognized that to be rooted in earth is not enough. He saw the need for man to breathe a spiritual air; and although he did not fully identify religion with its true source, God, he realized that it was, as much as the earth, a source of human development. Religion was, for him, the power of imaginative sensibility, transforming the primitive elements of the human root into a beautiful growth.

In all this, Hudson revealed that strange atavistic affinity with the primitive stages of individual and racial development to which I have already drawn attention. 'The whole mental régime of primitive man,' says Maritain, 'is contained under the primacy of the imagination. With him the intelligence is altogether bound up with and subordinate to the imagination. . . . Such a mental régime is one of experimental and lived connection with nature, of whose intensity and breadth we can only form a picture with difficulty.' And he adds that although 'an inferior condition' it is 'one in no way to be scorned. It is a human state, but a state of the childhood of humanity; a fruitful state, and a state through which it was necessary to pass' —that childlike condition to which I alluded in the previous chapter when considering Hudson's simple acceptance of life which flowers so perfectly in the 'second childhood' of the autobiography. Maritain further adds that in 'this régime humanity enriched itself with many vital truths, of which perhaps a great number were lost when it passed on to an adult state.' To these truths Hudson would recall us, not to regress but to go forward, embodying them in the consensus of modern knowledge and experience.

The simple life of sublimated imagination in harmony with nature advocated by Hudson would, if widespread, go far to check the pursuit of power to which all men are prone. The pursuit of power derives from self-conscious reasoning, and involves the force of will; and Hudson would have argued—indeed, the argument is implicit in all his work—that we can transcend our egoism only in an imaginative unity with nature. Where the imagination is satisfied the desire for power is no longer so urgently felt. Bertrand Russell seems to subscribe to the opposite view: in *Power : a New Social Analysis* he equates egoism with the driving force of the imagination. Now it is true that the imagination may play a part, but it more often sublimates the egoistic impulses. While recognizing that there is a negative egoism, an inverted power, that can proceed from the life of imaginative sensibility, I think that Hudson is on the right track.

In the transcendence of egoism, everything depends upon what is conceived to be the ultimate value. Now God alone is an Object great enough to transcend the ego; and any conception of the ultimate less than God—nation, class, man, art, nature—must, in the degree varying with the conception, fail. But Hudson, though he obviously suffered from the limitations imposed by his conception of nature as the ultimate value, did endeavour to go beyond it, and much of his work is a reaching out towards the transcendence of nature. This is not difficult to understand. Nature carries within itself a power of redemption from the grosser aspects of the self, a power that proceeds from its expression of the creative spirit and gives rise to the conception of 'a sacramental universe.' Distinguishing between the sacramental and the magical, Maritain writes that the latter operates 'in the nocturnal régime of imaginative thought, the former in the daylight régime of intellective thought'; but in Hudson, who retained something of the magical way of looking at nature along with the sacramental inheritance of Christianity, we have an approach that cannot satisfactorily be described as either magical or sacramental, yet includes both to some extent. As we saw in the first chapter, Hudson's outlook was *hylozoistic*—

the view that nature is alive, not in any particular aspect, but in its totality; and this involves both creatureliness and self-sufficiency in nature. For if nature has a self-sufficient, living principle of unity and wholeness, it follows that, as a whole is greater than its parts, the totality is, in some way that Hudson only dimly grasped, distinct from the parts; and in so far as he saw that the whole (which escapes our sensations and experience, but is implied in them) informs, and somehow shines through, the parts, nature was, for him, sacramental. At the same time, the *self-sufficiency* of nature is closely related to the magical conception of things exercising power in their own right.

The sacramental element contained in the notion of the whole, if logically followed, relates the universe to God. But Hudson was not a logical thinker, and such revelation of God as he received came from deep, and usually hidden, levels of intuition that he himself described as mystical. The mainspring of this mystical intuition was aesthetic; and as such it was interpreted by Hudson: not theistically. But in his search for beauty we can see a genuine groping after the holy, the numinous. The beauty which he sought, and with which he identified the wholeness of nature, was beyond any particular beautiful thing; beyond all art: it was, though he never fully realized it, that emanation of God of which St. Augustine spoke. 'Oh Beauty, ever old and ever new.' In the aesthetic wholeness of nature Hudson glimpsed the living God; for beauty can only be interpreted as one of the supreme manifestations of creativity. The mind plays its part in the reception of beauty; but that upon which the mind acts is objective. The philosophers who deny the objectivity of beauty and argue that it is in the beholder almost always give examples from nature. But where is the beauty in a work of art? We know that Bach arranged a certain number of notes in such a way as to communicate the experience called the Matthew Passion, and it is, of course, undeniable that what reaches the listener is a series of sound waves; but does this mean that he creates the beauty he hears? If so, he might as well forget about Bach and compliment himself upon his own genius. Manifestly this is absurd; and I contend that it is no less absurd to deny objectivity to the beauty of a sunset. To any one not inhibited by a particular metaphysical theory, the sunset is no more subjective than a composition by Bach or a painting by Rembrandt; and it seems to me only reasonable to hold that it is the work of a supreme creative mind. For Hudson, beauty seems to have been not so much created as *sui generis*—not in the Platonic sense, but as the essence or wholeness of nature. 'The sense of the beautiful is God's best gift to the soul,' he wrote in *Hampshire Days*. Few possess it fully, and in most of us it varies in intensity; and it is just this variety in the reactions of different people to beauty that has led to the subjectivist argument. Nevertheless, as Dr. Joad has pointed out, the fact that people coming into a room judge the temperature differently, one who is hot judging it cool, another who is cold judging it warm, does not alter the fact that there is an objective temperature registered on the thermometer. Neither does the fact that people differ about what is beautiful, and the degrees of beauty, prove that beauty is subjective.

In the *Hind*, Hudson argues that, though often atrophied, the sense of the beautiful is in us all, and in all creatures:

> When Santayana in his *Sense of Beauty* states that it is a small thing in our lives, and its outcome no more than the wild and pretty herbs that root themselves in granite mountains which represent the realities of our nature, I disagree with him and his simile. Beauty is not a casual growth, the result of a seed fallen from goodness knows where into a man's life; it is inherent in the granite itself, and another result from it is the development of a sense and impulse in the whole of life. It is in us all from birth to death—from the ant to the race of men: in the lowest and meanest of us. And it is in the animals, as we see from their games and music.

Hudson's last testament was a testament of beauty. For

him, the experience of earthly beauty was supreme; and it was in the presence of such beauty that certain rare and deeply treasured moments of mystical union came to him. Most of us, whatever our creed or outlook, have at some time or other experienced such moments, when the multiple and problematical aspects of life which bewilder us and wear down our daily existence, suddenly fall away, and we see the unity and purpose of life, and know, with Juliana of Norwich, that 'all shall be well, and all manner of things shall be well.' Hudson rarely spoke of his moments of illumination: like all such experiences they were indefinable; but sometimes we catch glimpses of them in the inspired passages of his books, and we have Roberts's testimony that he believed 'his own occasional uplift and communion with Nature' to be genuinely mystical. 'In his higher moments,' Roberts writes, 'the world and he were one.'

Aldous Huxley has called nature mysticism 'ersatz.' He stresses the fact that mysticism, in the sense of a deepening of consciousness, need not necessarily be genuine or even morally desirable: a man may invite such experiences 'for the sake of his nation, his party, his sect, or even the devil. In all these cases he will be given strength,' since 'a current flowing from the subliminal sea is in itself a tremendous force, even though this sea may remain cut off from the ocean of reality beyond it.' Elsewhere Huxley has described the effect of certain types of visual sensing in temporarily allaying self-consciousness; and he speaks of the curious physical identification of the observer with the seen when coming out of an anaesthetic. Now I suggest that in its lowest form, nature mysticism is just such a kind of physical identification: the self is lost not in God, but in generalized sensation. But I do not think this justly describes the quality of Hudson's experience, although it seems to have been the mode of his experiencing. At times, as when he writes of the sensation of floating with a field of wild flowers, he may have been experiencing a simple form of sense-identification; but Roberts says that 'in his higher moments *the world* and he were one.' In this unity with the whole, the nature mystic approximates to the genuine mysticism of the theocentric. Nature is the garment of God; and those who find Him in nature often come very close to the experience of the theocentric. Hudson did not seek mystical experience, but the exercise of his imaginative sensibility brought him, on rare occasions, into spontaneous relation with the 'subliminal sea,' and at such moments he saw, not God, but, as the words of his epitaph so happily expressed it, 'the brightness of the skirts of God.'

Hudson's devotion to nature integrated his outlook; but the rectitude of his life came from Christianity. He found no basis in nature for the kind of ethics he professed, and like so many agnostics of his age, he accepted, ready-made, the ethical system of Christianity. He lived an exceptionally full and happy life; but I believe that if he had embraced the complete spiritual-material unity of Christianity he would have lived even more fully and his vision have shone more brightly—for Christianity embraces nature in a higher synthesis, not deifying it, nor, like the oriental religions, dismissing it as illusory. The Christian unity of heaven and earth is summed up in the Incarnation, which unified the whole of creation. In becoming man, in assuming to Himself a human body, God also became, in an obscure but none the less real sense, nature; and thus, although we may reject the pantheistic conception that nature is God, there is a sense in which, in Christ, God is nature. The human body which God assumed in Christ is also the garment of earth and moon and sun and stars, and of the whole material universe; so that at the Incarnation nature became, in sober fact, the garment of God. For if the doctrine of physical evolution is true, the unity of the human body with nature is included in the higher unity of God with man, in Christ.

For long ages prior to the coming of Christ man had regarded nature as a thing alien and evil. The rebellion of the human will had brought disunity into the world. Man was cut off from God; and nature, darkened in the shadow of his darkness, had become an enemy peopled with the menacing forces of the human imagination—those forces which we still sometimes feel on ancient heaths and in deep forests. But with the coming of Christ, the old dark war was ended, and a new marriage of heaven and earth was made among men. The homeliness of the events of Bethlehem—the manger, the star, the shepherds—foreshadowed the intimacy with nature that flowered in the Middle Ages and received its greatest impetus from St. Francis of Assisi. We cannot understand the vision of St. Francis apart from his background. For him, the whole universe sang its canticle of canticles in joy of Christ who had united man, nature, and God. The great evolutionary cycle from nebula to man, from Brother Fire to Brother Ass, was transformed in the living Christ.

St. Francis did not know a single fact upon which the modern doctrine of evolution rests; but intuitively he grasped the unity of nature. With the passing of the medieval world the vision of St. Francis was partly lost. The material discoveries and development of capitalism and industrialism that originated from the Renaissance, and the subjectivism implicit in the Reformation, led men away from nature, the one externally, the other internally; and the growth of scepticism and the development of scientific materialism sundered the Christian unity of man, nature, and God, and gave us the rootless man of the modern age. Against all this, men such as Hudson rebelled; but the conception of nature had undergone a change. St. Francis had regarded nature as a brother, a little brother who had never quite grown up—hence his tolerance of 'nature red in tooth and claw,' an aspect that arouses emotions of scepticism and pessimism in the modern naturist. For St. Francis, nature was a younger brother born of a common father: for Hudson, nature was a beautiful, impersonal mother who took little thought for her children.

Few since the Reformation have integrated earth and heaven. Traherne came near to it, and his vision is very close to that of Hudson in the sense that, in Lawrence Housman's words, he 'definitely and joyously exalts the things of this world, and the delight of the senses'; but he went beyond Hudson 'by giving them a spiritual justification.' Housman observes how the Church has always denounced the Manichean heresy that would make out the material world as evil. 'Traherne insists that Christianity should stand for the enjoyment of life,' and according to him, the gospel 'is the enlargement and liberation of the senses in God's name'—a sentence that might well take its place as a footnote to the *Hind.* Wordsworth also glimpsed something of that tremendous unity which had been sundered by the twin evils of materialism and subjectivism: so also Jefferies, and many others. But perhaps the nearest approach to the old unity was found in the Catholic poets such as Francis Thompson and Hopkins. In Hopkins there is, at last, a genuine integration, though it is gained only at the price of a continual, emotional tension. That which Hudson lacked is found in *The Windhover*, dedicated 'To Christ Our Lord,' where Hopkins likens the flight of the kestrel and the soul's heavenward flight. In *Pied Beauty* Hopkins sings of the joys of earth in tones no less convinced than Hudson's, but with a deeper understanding:

Glory be to God for dappled things—
For skies of couple-colour as a brinded cow;
For rose-moles all in stipple upon trout that swim;
Fresh-firecoal chestnut-falls; finches' wings;
Landscape plotted and pieced—fold, fallow, and plough;
And áll trádes, their gear and tackle and trim.

All things counter, original, spare, strange;
Whatever is fickle, freckled (who knows how?)
With swift, slow; sweet, sour; adazzle, dim;
He fathers-forth whose beauty is past change:
Praise him.

Here, in the words of Charles Williams, is Hopkins's 'passionate sense of the details of the world without and the world within, a passionate consciousness of all kinds of experiences'; and this delight in the visible and invisible world, this power and richness of imagery, this love of whatever is 'counter, original, spare, *strange*' (the word that Hudson loved) was the poetic flowering of the Christian marriage of heaven and earth.

Man is rooted in earth and draws his breath from heaven; but to-day his roots are cut and his breath is stifled, and for the first time in the history of the world men have lost touch with both nature and God. 'We are bleeding at the roots, because we are cut off from the earth and sun and stars,' said Lawrence. But we are not only bleeding at the roots: we are sick and restless with an unsatisfied longing for the divine air by which we breathe. 'Thou hast made us for Thyself, and our hearts are restless until they find rest in Thee.' Conformity to nature and to the will of God are essential to human life, and each is related to the other. As T. S. Eliot has put it: 'We may say that religion, as distinguished from modern paganism, implies a life in conformity with nature. It may be observed that the natural life and the supernatural life have a conformity to each other which neither has with the mechanical life.' Modern civilization tends to be increasingly urban and atheistic, and to regard man as a system of reflexes conditioned by wireless, press, and cinema. Industrial man is denied contact with the earth no less than with the life of worship: the proletarian neither ploughs nor prays, and the beauty of nature and the glory of the house of God are alike alien to him. And because his roots are cut and his breath stifled, his thwarted energy expresses itself in war, revolution, economic crisis. The damming back of the two sources of human life isolates the individual and increases that threat to the ego which is the foundation of all neurosis. The whole fabric of industrial life produces instability and impoverishes the life of man. Its effects are the increasing superficiality of thought and fanatical violence of action that are summed up in the word totalitarianism.

Hudson died before the full tide of totalitarianism; but he saw it implicit in the movements of his time, and all his work is a tacit protest against it. He was not a revolutionary: he did not rage against the industrial world and seek to overthrow it: he offered us an alternative, the vision of earth. Massingham complained that he lacked religion; but there are men of unusual gifts who, in good faith, find integration in an ultimate value less than God. Of such was Hudson; and his justification is to be found in the words of the old countryman in one of Belloc's essays, who said that 'everything he saw was part of his own country, and that just as some holy men said that to be united with God, our Author, was the end and summit of man's effort, so to him who was not very holy, to mix and have communion with his own sky and earth was the one banquet that he knew. . . .' The banquet that Hudson spread for us is simple enough; but those who have sat down with him have not gone unfilled. For nature is one of the two great origins of our being that we have lost, and the way back, without which there is no life in us, is through such a vision as was vouchsafed to Hudson. There has never been a writer quite like him, nor will there ever be another: in the long history of English literature he was inimitable. The vision that shines from his pages is salutary for our time; and in the midst of crisis and revolution and the everlasting grind of 'the dark Satanic mills,' we shall find in his pages the peace and satisfaction that come from the highest art wedded to the most profound sensibility. Those who are without faith, the weary, the frivolous, the sceptical, the blind, will find there a better way of life; and those who walk in the light of faith will see a new vision, not of heaven only, but of earth at one with heaven, and indivisible.

INDEX

BIBLIOGRAPHY

A LIST of Hudson's Works (based on the Complete Works, in 24 volumes, published in a limited edition by J. M. Dent & Sons Ltd., 1924).

The Purple Land, 1885.

A Crystal Age, 1887.

The Naturalist in La Plata, 1892.

Fan: the Story of a Young Girl's Life (originally published as by 'Henry Harford'), 1892.

Idle Days in Patagonia, 1893.

British Birds, 1895.

Birds in London, 1898.

Nature in Downland, 1900.

Birds and Man, 1901.

El Ombú, with *The Story of a Piebald Horse*, *Pelino Viera's Confession*, *Nino Diablo*, *Marta Riquelme*, and *Ralph Herne*, 1902.

Hampshire Days, 1903.

Green Mansions, 1904.

A Little Boy Lost, together with the Poems, 1905.

The Land's End, 1908.

Afoot in England, 1909.

A Shepherd's Life, 1910.

Adventures among Birds, 1913.

Far Away and Long Ago, 1918.

Birds in Town and Village, 1919.

The Book of a Naturalist, 1919.

Birds of La Plata, 1920.

Dead Man's Plack, *An Old Thorn*, and *Miscellanea*, 1920.

A Traveller in Little Things, 1921.

A Hind in Richmond Park, 1922.

W. H. Hudson. A Portrait. By Morley Roberts. Nash & Grayson, 1924.

Semblanza de Hudson. By Fernando Pozzo. Instituto de Conferencias del Banco Municipal, Buenos Aires, 1940 (p. 37).

Essays on Hudson in various books, such as *Mightier than the Sword* by F. M. Ford; by C. E. M. Joad, H. J. Massingham, etc.

Letters from W. H. Hudson to Morley Roberts. Nash & Grayson, 1925.

Letters from W. H. Hudson to Edward Garnett. Dent, 1925.

A Hudson Anthology. Edited by Edward Garnett. Dent, 1924.

DATE DUE
